Phil Campion is a fifty-year-old veteran of military operations in just about every conflict-prone corner of the world, as a soldier in the regular Armed Forces, an elite operator and a mercenary. He continues to work as an operator on the private military circuit and lives with his partner, Wendy, on a houseboat in Norfolk. He is also a media commentator and best-selling author.

Also by Phil Campion

Born Fearless
Desert Fire
Killing Range
The Real World SAS Survival Guide

WHO DARES WINS

MY INSPIRATIONAL STORY FROM BROKEN
HOMES TO BATTLEFIELDS AND BEYOND

PHIL CAMPION

QUERCUS

First published in Great Britain in 2021 by Quercus.
This paperback edition published 2022 by

QUERCUS

Quercus Editions Ltd
Carmelite House
50 Victoria Embankment
London EC4Y 0DZ

An Hachette UK company

A CIP catalogue record for this book is available
from the British Library

MMP ISBN 978 1 52940 742 6
Ebook ISBN 978 1 52940 743 3

10 9 8 7 6 5 4 3 2 1

Typeset by CC Book Production
Printed and bound in Great Britain by Clays Ltd, Elcograf S.p.A.

MIX
Paper from
responsible sources
FSC® C104740

Papers used by Quercus are from well-managed forests and other responsible sources.

O Lord, who didst call on thy disciples to venture all to win all men to thee, grant that we, the chosen members of the Special Air Service Regiment, may by our works and our ways dare all to win all, and in so doing render special service to thee and our fellow men in all the world, through the same Jesus Christ our Lord.

The Regimental Collect, 22 SAS

TOMMY

I went into a public 'ouse to get a pint o' beer,
The publican 'e up an' sez, "We serve no red-coats here."
The girls be'ind the bar they laughed an' giggled fit to die,
I outs into the street again an' to myself sez I:
O it's Tommy this, an' Tommy that, an' "Tommy, go away";
But it's "Thank you, Mister Atkins," when the band begins to play
The band begins to play, my boys, the band begins to play,
O it's "Thank you, Mister Atkins," when the band begins to play.

I went into a theatre as sober as could be,
They gave a drunk civilian room, but 'adn't none for me;
They sent me to the gallery or round the music-'alls,
But when it comes to fightin', Lord! they'll shove me in the stalls!
For it's Tommy this, an' Tommy that, an' "Tommy, wait outside";
But it's "Special train for Atkins" when the trooper's on the tide
The troopship's on the tide, my boys, the troopship's on the tide,
O it's "Special train for Atkins" when the trooper's on the tide.

Yes, makin' mock o' uniforms that guard you while you sleep
Is cheaper than them uniforms, an' they're starvation cheap.
An' hustlin' drunken soldiers when they're goin' large a bit
Is five times better business than paradin' in full kit.
Then it's Tommy this, an' Tommy that, an' Tommy, 'ow's yer soul?"
But it's "Thin red line of 'eroes" when the drums begin to roll
The drums begin to roll, my boys, the drums begin to roll,
O it's "Thin red line of 'eroes," when the drums begin to roll.

We aren't no thin red 'eroes, nor we aren't no blackguards too,
But single men in barricks, most remarkable like you;
An' if sometimes our conduck isn't all your fancy paints,
Why, single men in barricks don't grow into plaster saints;
While it's Tommy this, an' Tommy that, an' Tommy, fall be'ind,"
But it's "Please to walk in front, sir," when there's trouble in the wind
There's trouble in the wind, my boys, there's trouble in the wind,
O it's "Please to walk in front, sir," when there's trouble in the wind.

You talk o' better food for us, an' schools, an' fires, an' all:
We'll wait for extry rations if you treat us rational.
Don't mess about the cook-room slops, but prove it to our face
The Widow's Uniform is not the soldier-man's disgrace.
For it's Tommy this, an' Tommy that, an' Chuck him out, the brute!"
But it's "Saviour of 'is country" when the guns begin to shoot;
An' it's Tommy this, an' Tommy that, an' anything you please;
An 'Tommy ain't a bloomin' fool – you bet that Tommy sees!

– Rudyard Kipling

Death before dishonour.

2Pac Shakur

AUTHOR'S NOTE

For reasons of operational security, and also for legal reasons, a number of personal names, dates, and place names have been changed, to protect people's identities and to properly obscure sensitive information, including the details of all the pupils at my school and all those I met in Africa.

This book has been written by myself, with the kind assistance of military author Damien Lewis, a man who, while never having served himself, is a passionate advocate of veteran's rights and a good and constant friend to the wider military community, as well as being an outstanding military historian in his own right. As such, it is a creative collaboration between the two of us. The fact Lewis spent two decades working as a reporter on the frontline of war means he and I can speak the same language; we can relate; we know what it's like to be under fire, or to face death repeatedly.

In the military in which I served, great emphasis was placed upon soldiers' honesty, integrity and the power of speaking the truth. We were encouraged to confess our wrongdoings and better ourselves. Many books such as this one are authored with some-what less than candid honesty, in my view, with former military men posing as the sole and only author. I did not write this book alone. However, it remains one hundred percent my story.

Rarely are two individuals' recollections of events the same and especially when concerning some of the frontline missions depicted in these pages. Nevertheless, I have endeavoured to portray a true and accurate account of what took place on the ground during the incidents depicted.

The above notwithstanding, the factual accuracy of the events portrayed herein remains the sole responsibility of the authors, who take full accountability for any inadvertent errors that may have been made. They will be happy to correct any such errors in future editions.

CONTENTS

CHAPTER ONE

THE PILGRIMS

The title of this book is not only about who dares to win on the battlefield; maybe not even chiefly that. Maybe it's more about who dares to win the battle within, which is infinitely more difficult and challenging. I've chosen to break the silence. After fifty-odd years. It hasn't been easy, but it is the first step to truly winning.

I'm forty-nine years old and I'm standing on a stage in front of some two hundred people, about to reveal some things about myself that I have never told anyone before, not ever, and not even to my nearest and dearest – to those in my life that I love. I never for one moment imagined I would talk about this even privately, let alone share it with an audience of complete strangers. But it's been bottled up inside me for so long – ever since I was a small child – that I know it's a case of now or never.

I'm standing before an audience of those who mostly work for local authorities and are responsible for fostering the kind of children whose lives were not dissimilar to my own; dysfunctional, traumatic, loveless and worse. They've come here expecting a motivational speech about how my childhood in care was a relative success, leading me to the place where I am today – a former elite forces soldier who has written bestselling books and made a career as something of a media personality. But the guy who spoke before me said something that triggered me; that made me tear up the script I'd prepared and step up to the lectern with no script at all; just a raw, burning desire to speak truth to power. A professional in the fostering field, the guy before me has told the story of one child who was subjected to horrific abuse while in the care system, and all because the authorities missed the signs, and mostly because no one spoke out about it, or at least not before it was way too late. Not until the damage had been well and truly done.

The conspiracy of silence *enabled* the abuse to continue – hidden, unchecked, spreading, worsening; like a horrific cancer. And that's triggered something inside of me. I can either be part of the problem – the conspiracy of silence – or I can choose to be part of the solution, which means *breaking the silence*. For the first time ever. Unthinkable, until now, this very moment, on this stage, provoked by the story of one kid condemned to be chained in the horrific darkness; the pit of abuse; a product of the system who, like me, died the death of a thousand cuts at the hands of those who should have been protecting and nurturing him; surrounding him with compassion and with love.

Sod it, what the hell – let's go for it; I'm ready.

Throwing caution and not a little fear to the wind, I lay aside the script I've prepared – my feelgood fluffy-bunny speech – and I lift my eyes to the audience and I prepare to take the plunge.

I begin by explaining how I had every intention of delivering the talk that they were all expecting, but that there's been something of a change of plan. What they're going to get will be spontaneous, unscripted, raw, but it's a far more important story and a very personal one. My voice tight with emotion, I give it to them like it is: I've not told anyone about any of this before, but I'm going to share it with them now. This is not what this audience were expecting, and it seems to have more than grabbed their attention. As I pause, plucking up the courage to leap into the dirt and the darkness, I sense the tense and expectant silence that has settled across the hall.

I start off by telling them that I was interfered with as a child in a series of children's homes across the south of England, and that I had some truly horrendous stuff inflicted on me by people in positions of authority and trust, who were in reality twisted sexual predators. One individual, a supposedly 'respectable' married man with children of his own, turned out to be the worst abuser of all. Everyone looked up to him like he was some kind of superhero – including me – but behind the façade he was using children for his own sick and perverted ends.

At this point, you could hear a pin drop; the room has gone completely quiet, everyone's jaw seeming to drop open. I'm well aware of what they were expecting to hear: my 'agreed' script had me talking about how I went through the care system, was fostered, was adopted and wow, wasn't it wonderful how it saved my life, and just look where I am today. But the truth is – that is a lie. A convenient script that plays well. The truth is so very, very different. The truth is, it was awful and hellish beyond any words I have in my head to say, and it nearly destroyed me. And the truth is, it's haunted me until this day, and still does.

And sod it, that's exactly what they're going to hear.

I start to lay out the bare bones of my story to the hushed audience, and I am determined to hide absolutely nothing. I was the second child of an unmarried couple, Della and Martin Smith, who christened me Wayne. Wayne Smith. They already had the one son and when I came along, things got too much for Martin and he left home. Della was now faced with juggling single-parenthood, work and a new-born baby boy, plus a toddler, and she was simply overwhelmed. At six months of age I was put up for adoption.

My new – adoptive – parents were Audrey and Alan Campion. They already had an adopted daughter, called Anne, and they lived in a small semi on a rough and ready council estate in Southampton. Audrey had given up work to look after Anne, while Alan had recently been suspended without pay from his job shunting trains around the Southampton docks. He'd been accused of running a cigarette-smuggling racket with the ship's crews.

With their delusions of grandeur, Audrey and Alan decided to rename me Philip Lewis Alexander Campion, a name far more in keeping with their social aspirations, for in their view I was going to be the adopted son of respectable church-going, middle-class folks. But in truth, with no money coming in we weren't going anywhere – least of all climbing the social ladder or getting off that dog-rough estate. It wasn't long before Alan – unable to deal with his frustrations regarding the lack of work and the lack of cash to fund the lifestyle to which they aspired – started to take it out on me, using Philip Lewis Alexander Campion – a toddler – as his punchbag.

While my increasingly violent 'father' dished out regular

beatings, Audrey just stood by and let it happen. It was as if she viewed it all as my fault and that I somehow deserved to get beaten up. As Alan's jobless state dragged on and on, tensions at 'home' kept escalating and soon he began taking his anger out on Audrey, too. Eventually, she could take no more. Audrey divorced Alan and took Anne and me with her.

Life improved for a little while, but then Audrey began experiencing deep depression. She would disappear and go missing for days on end. The police would eventually find her wandering around in nearby woodland, where she'd attempted to commit suicide. Audrey's mental health started to spiral downwards fast, and she turned violent towards me. I wasn't prepared to stand by and take another beating, and so I decided to fight back.

It seemed to work and things quietened down, at least for a while. But Audrey alighted upon another strategy to make my life hell: she took to cutting my hair so that I was left with a floppy fringe that made me look like an effeminate choir-boy; in truth, the kind of son that, in her delusions, she was trying to convince herself she really had. Not content with all that, she began dressing me in a combination of flowery shirts and tweedy jackets, which left me looking a complete Hooray-Henry twit. It would have been just about okay in Kensington or Mayfair; but not on Southampton's Harefield Estate.

When I turned up at my comprehensive school – one composed of largely working-class kids – I was teased, mocked and hunted mercilessly. No surprises there. I told Audrey about the bullying, but she just said that I should turn the other cheek or run away. At first, I followed her advice. I was young, she was the only 'parental' figure I had ever had and I knew no better. But then I was labelled a coward and the bullying just got worse.

Eventually, I realised I had only two choices: either to keep taking the beatings or to fight back. I wasn't prepared to stand by and accept any more punches or kickings from the gang of school toughs, so I retaliated. Over time, I learned to give as good as I got and to take the bullies on. Bullies are basically small-minded cowards who always back down when fronted out. But back at home, my relationship with Audrey just kept worsening.

It was clear that I was a burden she didn't want. I was constantly hungry because she fed me so little. I even ended up eating the food she put down for the cats. The only other choice I had was to earn what I could legally, doing paper rounds, and to steal whatever else I could get my hands on. The money was used to buy extra food like fish and chips, in an effort to stave off the hunger.

One time I got caught stealing some of the takings from my paper-round and I ended up in court. It was the final straw for Audrey, who accused me of bringing 'shame' on the family. I fired back at her that she was a hopeless example of a mother who couldn't even feed me properly. Eventually, social services intervened, due to my near-starvation. Finally someone at my school had felt they couldn't turn a blind eye anymore to the famished, skinny kid who was too crazed with hunger to concentrate on his studies.

I was taken out of Audrey's 'care' and put into a children's reception centre, called Willow Lodge, in Southampton. I had to stay there while they decided what to do with me. From the very start I loathed being locked up, which was pretty much what happened at Willow Lodge. After the first few weeks, I ran away and lived rough in the local woods. I scavenged whatever I could find by rooting through dustbins, while taking clothes off washing lines to stay warm.

I made friends with another lad from Willow Lodge, called Sam. Together we would abscond and live on the streets for weeks on end. When it came to nightfall, we'd walk the railway line until we came to a rail worker's hut, and sneak inside to shelter from the cold. If we were lucky, we might find some thick donkey jackets left behind by the workers, or even a coal-burning stove that was still warm.

Due to our regular absconding, Sam and I were moved from Willow Lodge to Lakeside Lodge, a 'secure' facility. By now we were twelve years old. With bars on the windows, the authorities hoped they could put a stop to our regular break-outs, but it only made us more determined, especially because at Lakeside Lodge we had our first experience of the sexual predators.

In those days there was little or no vetting of staff or visitors, and it soon became apparent that two men who were around regularly were up to no good. Every evening, before bedtime, they'd start their rounds by checking down each boy's pyjamas, to 'ensure their pants had been removed before going to bed'. Or so they claimed.

They used the pathetic excuse that they were doing this to protect a boy's manhood, claiming, 'Your willy won't grow properly if you keep your pants on.' Of course, it was just an excuse to have a good feel of some of the boys. But the really frightening thing, looking back on it now was that I didn't feel like I could tell anybody about this kind of stuff. As I explained to the audience that I was revealing all of this to in that Birmingham conference hall, there was absolutely no one a kid like me in a home like that could confide in. No one at all.

The gropers made it very clear that this was just what happened at Lakeside Lodge. It was the norm; it went with the territory. The only people we could possibly confide in were our peers. Sam and I decided we'd just keep our mouths shut, because who would listen to the likes of us? I'd been told since I was old enough to understand that I was a nothing; a low-life; a scrote. If adults tell a child something for long enough, he or she will believe it as if it's gospel. But Sam and I were still old enough and wise enough to know the difference between right and wrong, and what the gropers were doing was wrong.

I was determined not to take any such shit myself, but some of the younger kids would be like startled rabbits in the headlights and just freeze, as the two gropers did their nightly rounds. There was a child in there who had significant learning disabilities, and goodness only knows what they put that poor guy through. At the end of the day, there were only two choices as I saw it: either I went with it, and accepted the night time predations, if they decided to start with me or I fought against it. It was the lesson from my earliest days at comprehensive school, all over again.

One of the first things that I'd learned at Lakeside Lodge was to always try to get a positive out of a negative. It sounds pretty awful, but I would try to crack a joke about the abuse. 'Well, if you close your eyes and pretend it's a bird with their hands down your pants, it's not so bad.' We had to find humour in it, to stay sane – to get through. But only for so long . . .

Standing up to the gropers was probably the hardest thing I'd ever done, because they had made it very clear: if you didn't go along with what they said and accept what they did to you, they'd make your life intolerable. In other words – your life may be shit now, but we're going to make it double-shit if you object or complain. There are not many kids who will decide in such a situation: *Okay, I'll have a dose of double shit then.* In fact, I ended up having to be devious myself to survive in such a horrific situation.

One night I hid a thick wooden bed-leg under my sheets, where I knew the gropers wouldn't see it. When the first one came and tried to feel me up, I unleashed hell, smashing him repeatedly over the head, all my pent-up rage against the system and the horror and despair at the sheer bloody betrayal of it all flooding out in a paroxysm of violence and rage. The next morning, the incoming staff were told the Groper's injuries had been caused by an accident, and without anyone to say any different how were they to know otherwise.

I didn't get into trouble, because the gropers knew what would happen if what they were up to got out. The result was that a macabre, unspoken agreement developed between them and me. If I kept quiet about the Lakeside Lodge gropers, I'd earn my freedom from such abuse. We had reached an unholy understanding: they'd leave me alone, if I left them alone, and that meant turning a blind eye to what they did to the others. The one positive that came out of it was that from then on they kept their distance.

What choice did I have but to go along with that kind of a deal? What other option was there? I was just trying to survive, a teenage kid alone, with no family or loved ones to care for me, or to look out for me, or to confide in, and knowing fully well that here, where I was supposed to be being looked after, I was at the mercy of those who were in truth abusers. Me and dozens of other young and vulnerable children were being preyed upon by sick and twisted sexual predators . . .

I took a pause in my talk, and I could see row upon row of faces staring back at me, with expressions that were utterly frozen; gripped. Here they were getting what they had least expected, the inside story from the victim of the kind of abuse it was their job to prevent, and from the most unexpected of sources – elite military veteran, bodyguard to the stars and motivational speaker, Phil Campion. But in truth, I hadn't even got started yet.

With all the trouble I'd been getting into, I was appointed a social worker, Dianne Ferry, who came to visit me regularly. I got on well with her and trusted her, or at least as much as I trusted anyone right then. She genuinely seemed to want to help. She was trying to find a foster parent willing to take me on, but who was going to invite into their home a messed-up bundle of anger and resentment and a feral absconder like me?

I'd been expelled from my comprehensive school, and Dianne came to see me offering some potentially good news. She'd got me to complete various IQ tests, proving that I was smart and capable intellectually, and from her experience she certainly knew I was resourceful. She figured I just needed a second-chance and the right environment in which to thrive. It turned out that she had persuaded the authorities to offer me a government-sponsored place at an exclusive private boarding school, called Kingham Hill.

This was going to be my ticket into a new life, Dianne promised me. Kingham Hill was about as far as you could get from my council-estate upbringing. A grand country mansion set in acres of open countryside in leafy and genteel Oxfordshire, it had everything money could buy or any school kid could wish for: acres and acres of immaculate lawns, a massive indoor swimming pool, riding stables, a billiard-table-flat cricket pitch, and even an enormous drama theatre that included a real stage.

It was a dream opportunity, but as it turned out it wasn't going to prove any kind of dream, or at least not for the likes of me. From the very outset I didn't fit in. I didn't dress the same, I didn't speak the same and I wasn't paying my way to be there. Everyone else was seriously wealthy and had been through the same exclusive prep school system, yet there was I, the comprehensive school kid from a council-estate who just turned up half-way through term, out of the blue. I stuck out like a bulldog's nuts.

I'd had it instilled into me that I had to make my mark right from the start, to let my peers know I wasn't going to be pushed around; that I wasn't daunted or scared. The first day at Kingham Hill, one of the lads, Anthony, asked me if I'd like to join them for a smoke behind Greenwich House. When we got there, one of the other lads started to abuse me verbally. Anthony turned to me and said: 'Are you going to stand for that? Why don't you go and hit him?' It was like being back in junior school, faced by the gangs of bullies. *Show fear and you're finished.* I needed them to know I wasn't frightened, so I walked over and punched the kid who was abusing me right in the face.

After that the Kingham Hill nasties kept their distance, but it didn't stop them from taunting me verbally, whenever they felt they could get away with it. We spent a week in Belgium, on a cycling trip to visit the Allied war graves. I felt so utterly isolated. All the others had their own little cliques, and they made it perfectly clear that I wasn't a part of any of them. Even the teachers seemed to keep their distance, like I was a leper or something. We had a group photograph at the end of the trip, and if you look closely you'll see I'm actually sticking my middle finger up to the camera.

That pretty much sums up what I felt at Kingham Hill: *screw you*.

None of us really understood the significance of what we were seeing, when we visited the war graves. We were thirteen, without much of a care for anyone but ourselves. All I wanted to do was ride my bike and mess around and to *fit in*. Somewhere, surely somewhere, I could fit in. *Find a home*. I looked at all the names of the fallen inscribed on the iron gates and the stone monuments and on the serried ranks of the gravestones and thought – *yeah, whatever*. It meant nothing to me.

It wasn't until I went back years later, after serving my time in the military, that I began to appreciate what those memorials actually signified. Having seen the devastation of war up close, when I looked at the names of the fallen and their ages it really hit home – there were a vast number of young men who had been struck down in their prime, in freedom's cause. That would be a hugely emotional time for me. The Kingham Hill visit was too, but for entirely different reasons – ones of exclusion, rejection and betrayal.

On returning to school, the teasing continued remorselessly, until one day the inevitable happened and I snapped. One of the posh bully-boys, Cornelius, had been taunting me for weeks on end, constantly reminding me of all the reasons why I shouldn't be at a place like Kingham Hill. I was 'Kevin from the council-estate'. They'd nicknamed me 'Kevin'. Apparently, it's a common-as-muck name. I didn't have the right kind of background or upbringing or breeding. I was a dirt-poor, common-as-muck piece of shit, who was only there as a guest of the welfare state. On charity. An impostor. A loser. A fake. On this day, I decided I just couldn't take any more.

I walked into the boot room – where the pupils kept their out-door shoes – removed the heavy metal floor buffer, returned to the library where Cornelius had been needling me, and without further ado I smashed the heavy buffer over his head. All the rage and frustration that had been building up inside me following the months of teasing and verbal abuse suddenly exploded. Erupting in a raging hurricane of resentment and violent rage, I drove everyone out of the library, barricading myself inside, and challenging anyone with the balls to stand and fight 'Council House Kevin'.

Needless to say, it was curtains for me at Kingham Hill. I was summarily removed, expelled and sent to George Buildings, a top-security centre where the unruliest of kids-in-care are incarcerated. Eventually, the authorities found me a more permanent place, within a Church of England-sponsored kids' home set in a green and leafy and heavily-wooded part of southern England. It didn't stop me from absconding, though, and for the first few days I lived rough in the woods.

But gradually, at this new place I began to sense that the staff seemed different and somehow more understanding. For the first time I sensed I might have found somewhere I might fit in. Situated alongside the kids' home there was a small education unit run by a guy in his late thirties, called Terry Houlihan, who had been a headmaster at a previous school. He also worked at a nearby activities and outdoor pursuits centre, where he taught canoeing and was the chief ski instructor. Everyone loved Terry. He was fun and cool, and a really likeable sort of bloke. Or so I thought.

Terry seemed to look out for me and the other kids. If I was having a hard time, he'd take me back to his home for a night, just to get me out of the way of any trouble. His wife was really kind and he'd even bring his young children into the mix, so we'd spend time having fun and playing together. I guess it was my first experience of what I thought was a normal, loving family.

Terry was the sort of guy who would do anything for anybody. All of the staff and the kids seemed to love him, and during the first six months that I was at that new home his presence helped restore my faith in adults. Terry became one of the few people I really trusted. There was absolutely nothing he wouldn't do for me, or so I thought. In many ways, Terry became like the father that I had always wanted, but had never had.

But not for long.

CHAPTER TWO

TERRY THE BASTARD

One evening, after I'd had a day of particular aggravation and angst with various people in the home, Terry said to me: 'Why don't you come around to my place, Phil? I'm going home in about an hour's time. We can have a cup of tea and you can get away for a bit.'

He only lived a short distance down the road, so it was easy to catch a bus there. I knocked on the front door and I heard somebody call out: 'It's open. Come in.'

It wasn't unusual for Terry to call you in like that, so I just pushed the door open and walked inside. The front door led into a lounge, but when I went in all the curtains were drawn, which was odd. It was so dark I couldn't see Terry anywhere, but I heard him call out: 'Come on in, Phil, sit down.'

I felt a bit uncomfortable, but this was Terry, after all. My father figure. My saviour. *My hero.*

I sat down on one of the armchairs. As my eyes adjusted to the gloom, I could see a figure standing in one corner of the room and he had no top on. It was Terry, and when I looked closer I realised he had nothing on at all. He was stark bollock naked. I was so shocked I was utterly rooted to the spot. My mind kept telling me that this could not be happening. No way could this be

15

happening. It had to be some mistake. Maybe he'd just come out of the shower and was on the way to change into some clothes. Surely, he had to be.

Terry took a step closer to me and began speaking: 'You know something, Phil, your behaviour's been shocking just lately. You've been really poorly behaved and this is one of my remedial tactics. This is how I show children how things can be put right. We're building up some trust here . . . But this is strictly between me and you, okay? Your problems can be sorted. 'Course your problems can be fixed. I can help you. Together, we can find a solution, but we've got to build up this trust thing. So, you've gotta trust what I do now. But if you don't, if you say anything to anyone . . .'

I sat there horrified, absolutely horrified, as Terry, in the most twisted and sick way imaginable, proceeded to make it crystal clear that I was the scum of the earth, and that if I so much as breathed a word about what he was about to do, he would tell everybody that I had done X, Y and Z, and that I would be locked up in borstal or worse, and the authorities would throw away the key.

I was in total shock; I was in an impossible situation. I knew how many people respected Terry. *Everyone did.* They just wouldn't believe he could be capable of this, and especially if it was my word against his. All it would take was one phone call from Terry, and I'd be in a whole world of trouble. No one would ever think to listen to, let alone believe a powerless low-life serial absconder like me.

So, I stayed there, rooted to the armchair, my skin crawling, as he moved closer still. Then I heard a horribly familiar sound: Terry was standing there right behind me, wanking himself off.

16

As he did so, he kept saying to me: 'Don't say anything. Not a word. Now tell me, would you like to come and hold this? Come on, you would, wouldn't you?'

'No,' I managed to retort. 'I don't want nothing to do with it. I don't want to look at it even.'

He carried on doing what he was doing, and as he did so he kept reminding me of our relative positions – that he was a god, and I was a total, absolute nothing; the lowest of the low. I could tell he was getting off on this power trip; on the sheer unadulterated abuse of it all. And he kept saying to me: 'Come on. Come and touch it. Come and touch it. Come and touch it.'

I was fourteen years old. Before this moment, Terry had been like a god to me. Now I was starting to realise how wrong a teenage kid in care like me could be.

I kept telling him that no, I would not touch his thing. But he kept doing what he was doing and trying to draw me in. Eventually, it came to an end in a predictable and revolting way. I was still sitting there, riveted to the spot in horror and disgust. It suddenly occurred to me that I was like one of those younger kids had been, at Lakeside Lodge, when faced by the gropers. I was like a startled rabbit in the headlights, totally frozen in shock.

Terry proceeded to mop himself up, pulled up his tracksuit bottoms and put on his T-shirt, as if nothing particularly untoward had happened. As if this was a regular occurrence in his play book. He opened the curtains, turned to me and said: 'Right, we'd better get you back then, hadn't we?'

'I don't want a lift from you,' I retorted.

'No, no, no, you're not going to be like that,' he warned me.

'And you won't say anything, will you, Phil? You're not going to say anything at all. You're not going to do anything that might get you deeper into trouble, are you?'

It was all so utterly disgusting. I felt dirty. Dirtied. I wanted to leave of my own accord and get away, but he kept reminding me of the consequences if I didn't go back with him. In the end he got his way, because he said that if I didn't agree to go with him, he'd tell people that I'd absconded. He threatened that I'd be in a whole world of trouble, because he'd plant valuables on me and claim that I'd been caught stealing them from his home.

He drove me back to the kids' home, and in full earshot of everyone did his perfect Terry-the-hero act: 'Oh, great to see you Phil, great to see you. Thanks for coming round. Anytime. Anytime you need a hand, just let me know.' He then strolled into the staff room, and began talking loudly about how he'd done his good Samaritan bit with me. It was all so shocking and sickening, especially as Terry was so utterly convincing.

I was now in a position where I couldn't say anything to any of the other kids about what had happened, for fear of ridicule, or of them grassing me up and getting me into the kind of trouble Terry had threatened me with. Which, of course, I believed would be the outcome if I chose to take on a man of Terry's stature and repute. It was all such a horrific mess.

This happened two or three further times, before it got to the stage where I just wanted to leave. My behaviour nose-dived, but every time I did something wrong Terry-the-bastard would step in and announce: 'No, no, no, give him another chance.' And through no fault of their own the staff generally went with it – because

Terry was just so good at acting the great saviour-hero. For me this was the worst yet: I felt totally, utterly trapped. I had never felt so low; borderline suicidal.

I desperately wanted to get thrown out of the place, so my behaviour kept deteriorating. Of course, this was my cry for help. The only way I knew how. But every time I smashed something up or had a fight, Terry-the-bastard would find a way to intervene and say: 'Just give him another chance. I see something in this kid. He's a great kid.'

A few weeks later, Terry organized a kayaking trip for me and this other lad, who was a similar age to me and also had a history of life-in-care. I only agreed to go because of Terry's threats – threats that I believed would be carried out should I try to expose him – and because the other lad came across as being a really stand-up, smart kid. So it was that the three of us set off in Terry's car for the picture-postcard-perfect seaside town of Union Hall, in County Cork, Ireland.

It didn't take long for me to discover that what had happened to me had also happened to this other lad, only worse. He'd been preyed on so badly by Terry, that he'd actually done stuff with him. Worse still, when we got to Union Hall, set on the rugged and wild West Cork coastline, I found they were sharing a bedroom in the guest house, and that I was billeted in the room opposite. One night we all got pissed in this local bar, sinking pints of silky-smooth Irish Guinness, after which the two of them tried to drag me physically back to their room.

I fought the both of them off. I was having none of it. I made such a ruckus in the guest house that they had to let me go.

Another night the same thing began happening, only this time we ended up having a brawl on the street, that was until Terry realised how much attention he was drawing to himself and his dark perversions. Even during the day, I couldn't get away from him. Due to atrocious sea conditions – a dark storm had blown in, and it sat brooding over the Irish coastline for days on end – we couldn't do any kayaking until just before we left, which meant we were forced to keep off the water. I'd hoped that if I could get out on the sea in my own boat, that would at least prevent Terry from trying to drag me into his sick clutches. As it was, it was an utter nightmare.

Eventually, just before my sixteenth birthday, I managed to get out of that children's home and I went to live in a transport café. I finally had some independence and hoped I'd seen the back of Terry for good. But it wasn't long before he found out where I was living, and he started turning up unannounced and trying to lure me into his car.

One time he concocted a story that he was partly responsible for looking after me, and he managed to persuade the café staff to let him through to my accommodation at the rear. I heard a knock at the door and opened it, only to find him standing there. He told me that if I didn't go with him and back up his story, he'd have me thrown out of there and I'd be homeless. No matter where I went, he was hunting me, pursuing me; stalking me. Always delivering the same ultimatum; the same threat: *You're nothing. You're an utter lowlife. Speak out and you're finished.*

Terry was totally relentless and he began to make my life a misery all over again. I began a youth training scheme to become a ski instructor, which offered the first bit of financial security that I'd ever had. But Terry managed to put all that in jeopardy too. Every few weeks he'd turn up, trying to wank off in front of me or persuade me to touch him. Each time, I told myself that I had to report him, but every time he would come up with the same old powerful arguments as to why I couldn't. He told me I'd lose my job and my home, and that I'd be in major trouble with the police. I felt cornered: this one man who I'd once thought so much of was making my life a living hell.

Finally, with the youth training scheme coming to an end, I had to decide what to do with my life. I had hoped I could stay on at the activity centre but the guy who ran it, an ex-military type, told me he didn't have a place for me. He and two other guys who worked there came and had words with me, and they all tried to convince me that I should try for a career in the British military. For the avoidance of doubt, neither of them was my abuser, Terry Houlihan. Eventually, the guy who was ex-military himself offered to arrange for me to go down to the Army Career's Office, for an interview. I went, never thinking for one moment that they'd want to recruit someone like me. After years of being told I was nothing by the likes of Terry, I believed it. I had become a product of the system.

So, when the Army recruiting officer told me I was going to make it fine, and that the infantry was for me, I was gobsmacked. I was over the moon that they'd even take me, especially as the only qualification I had to my name was a cycling proficiency certificate. Once I was on the bus – off to join the Army proper – I felt overwhelmed by this massive sense of relief. For the first time,

I would be beyond Terry-the-bastard's reach. He couldn't come onto the Army camp to harass me, for all the obvious reasons. There was nothing more he could do to me. I was finally rid of the curse, for good. Or so I told myself at the time . . .

I did return, several years later, to the area where Terry had made my life a living hell, only to find that he was still living there. By this time, though, things had changed markedly. His wife had discovered his horrific, predatory behaviour and kicked him out of the family home. I had a feeling that sooner or later Terry's chickens would come home to roost, and sure enough they did. I found out some time later that he had moved in with another woman. The mother had found out and grassed him up to the police. Finally, Terry-the-bastard was charged and convicted.

And that, I concluded, was my story of abuse within the British care system – rounding off my impromptu talk. I mentioned the blindingly obvious – that I am six-foot tall and built like the proverbial barn door. I have fists like shovels. I've served in elite military units and lived by their mottos and their values: *death before dishonour*. I've taken my elite soldiering skills into many a war-torn corner of the world and taken few prisoners while there. Which just goes to show that even the toughest amongst us can get abused, secretly, seemingly without end, amidst a system that lets the most vulnerable suffer for years and years.

The minute I finished speaking, there was an absolute stillness and hush in the room. It was as if everyone was just sitting there not knowing what on earth to say. I could hear more than a few individuals sobbing. My story had brought them to tears. I thought to myself then: *Jesus, I wasn't quite expecting that.* My deeply personal, shocking story – one that I had never had the courage to fully reveal before – had really touched these people, who were widely-experienced in the care system. It had moved everyone in that room. In fact, it had stunned them all into a speechless quiet.

As I mingled for drinks afterwards, it became clear that I'd hit a real nerve – with the audience, and with myself, of course. I had opened a door to a part of me that I'd kept under lock and key for a very long time. It was a dark period of my life that I had never thought I'd reveal to anyone, let alone an audience of two-hundred unsuspecting souls. I just hoped that what I'd said would make a difference and help prevent other children from suffering what I had had to endure.

When I left the venue, I felt like a huge burden had been lifted from my shoulders. For the first time in my life, I finally felt free of the whole sordid episode.

By rights I should have hunted Terry-the-bastard down to the ends of the earth, and denounced him at the time. Since speaking out, very good friends have asked me: 'Well, why didn't you say anything when it happened?' The honest answer is that the pressures that I was put under back then made it impossible. According to some people I should have gone after him, but what would have been the point? Terry has been exposed for who and what he is, and has since passed away.

For years I'd been haunted by the demons of the past, and eventually they'd broke free. But back then, when as a teenage kid I had finally escaped from Terry's abusive clutches, all I wanted was to put that horrific episode of my life as far to the back of my mind as was possible, so that I never had to talk about it to anybody, ever. I wasn't about to let anyone or anything destroy the life that I was trying so hard to make for myself.

A life forged in the heat and the fire of the British military.

CHAPTER THREE

GREEN ARMY

It was the sort of weather that was perfect for late August in Africa: warm and balmy by day and cool enough to sleep at night. I was in my element engaged on training exercises in bush and jungle warfare with the rest of the lads of my unit. *Train hard, fight easy* has always been one of my favourite mantras. It was one I was to put to the test right now, as a corporal serving with the Royal Hampshires who was not yet nineteen years of age.

It was barely two years after I'd slipped Terry-the-bastard's clutches when I arrived in Kenya, in East Africa, with the Royal Hampshires (shortly to be renamed the Princess of Wales's Royal Regiment – the PWRR). Our instructors were SAS and unlike any soldiers that I'd ever met. With their long hair, beards and a relaxed professionalism they exuded pure competence and confidence. They didn't need to execute a great big song and dance of shouting and screaming to exert their authority. They spoke with a quiet assurance, knowing they were the best and that others would listen.

I was awestruck.

For the first time in the military, certainly, I was treated almost as an equal, and it was from them that I learned that invaluable secret to good soldiering: *train hard, fight easy.*

We'd flown in on a big ageing DC10 airliner and touched down in the capital, Nairobi. Even though we were slated to deploy to Northern Ireland, we still had to maintain our all-round soldiering skills, of which jungle warfare is arguably the ultimate test.

They say you either love or hate the jungle. It can be a harsh, fierce and unforgiving environment with the weather, climate and terrain always against you. Plus, there are insects crawling all over you 24/7, and everything else in the jungle basically wants you to eat you or kill you. Certainly, you can't hide your inadequacies and you can't bluff your way out. It's where your true qualities are revealed, for better or for worse. If a soldier can soldier in the jungle, he can soldier pretty much anywhere.

The minute we stepped off the DC10 the intense Kenyan heat hit us like a giant oven door had just been opened. We moved north and overnighted in the makeshift battalion HQ, at Nanyuki Showground, before heading into the bush the next day. After a long drive we arrived in an African village shortly before dusk, where we were introduced to our SAS instructors. Talk about a breath of fresh air . . . With their easy-going but focused attitude, I thought they were top drawer.

I listened with rapt attention as they outlined why the jungle is different and so very special . . . The reason you learn how to operate in such an environment is because it takes soldiering back to its very basics, and in one of the harshest environments known to man. At the end of the day elite soldiering comes down to building on the basic skills, plus developing the key qualities of self-discipline, integrity and reliability. Those SAS instructors were dead right: the building blocks for everything that I would do in elite forces would be my Green Army days. That was when and where the foundation was laid.

In the jungle, if you ignore the essentials, even in regard to your own health and hygiene, and you don't ensure the basics are done well, everything falls apart. Disregard the basics and it will come back to bite you on the arse. Because the jungle can be so all-consuming, you might tell yourself: *Oh, I won't bother changing my boots. I won't bother powdering my feet today.* You might leave it that extra 24 hours. But that's ignoring the absolute basics, and you'll end up with sores on your feet and need to be casevaced out of there.

You might take the attitude: *Oh, I won't get into my dry kit tonight.* (You have to keep two separate sets of clothing: a wet kit, to trek in during the day, and a dry one to sleep in at night). But you'll pay the price if you do, and you'll feel the ill-effects. If you can't do things properly in the jungle, you'll be forced out pretty promptly. If you're not fit to soldier in such a harsh environment, you'll die if you don't get out quickly enough – it's as simple as that.

During our first few days training there was a level of anticipation among all of us about exactly how difficult it was going to be. Obviously, we'd all heard horror stories about guys not making it through the jungle, or even dying. There was one tale doing the rounds about a guy who was charged by an elephant and trampled underfoot; another about a guy being hit by a tree which inexplicably collapsed during the night, crashing down onto his *basha* (his jungle shelter). It brought home to us that the jungle is an environment that can snuff you out, just like that.

We were given four or five days to acclimatise, before commencing anything too rigorous. There are two reasons for this. First, you don't want people collapsing in the jungle through heat exhaustion or dehydration. Secondly, once you're in the impenetrable heart of the deep forest, it's so close and dense under the canopy that you physically cannot see one another, so you may well have no idea where anyone else is or what they're up to. You need to know how to orientate yourself, taking into account those around you, before everyone heads into the clutches of the jungle proper.

After those few days' acclimatisation, we set off for the real thing. Although we weren't waiting to jump into an African village to start a fire-fight for real, there was still a level of anticipation; a level of expectation that we were going to have to switch on in this environment, or we weren't going to make it through.

We caught a truck which took us deep into the forest. First off it was a kind of dry bush-type environment, but the further we travelled the hotter and more humid it became and the thicker and more tangled and dense grew the vegetation. Eventually, we were in the midst of this primary jungle. I stared at the thick wall of vegetation to either side of us, thinking to myself: *this is awesome*.

As I got off the truck, the first thing that struck me was the heat. But as I moved out of the open into the trees, I stepped into an even hotter, boiling cauldron, which had an added sense of wetness to it – the intense humidity of the jungle. I hadn't felt it on the back of the truck so much, because we'd been roaring along with the wind catching us through the open sides. But once we were beneath the canopy proper, it was as if all the oxygen had been sucked out of the air.

28

The second thing I noticed was the incredible noises. There was every kind of whistling, whirring, pinging and chattering thing moving among the trees – insects flapping, buzzing, scratching and twitching all around us. It was a crazy cacophony of sound. You could fly over the jungle for a hundred years and you would never get a sense of the intense heat and the noise you experience once your feet are on the ground.

I remember humping my Bergen onto my back. It now felt insanely heavy, as did my belt kit around my waist and my weapon, as we started walking up a thin path that snaked through the dark trees. It was one of the steepest I've ever climbed in my life, and it proved a real tester as an initiation into the jungle. I couldn't even see the guy in front of me, because he was so much higher than me, that's how steep it was. Four or five steps up this absurdly precipitous hill and I was already soaked in sweat from head to toe and totally immersed in the hypnotic ambience of the jungle.

I was thinking to myself: *We've only just started up this track. If it's like this on the first day, God help us for the days to come.* You can only move extremely slowly in such a tropical environment, because of the heat and the resulting exhaustion. The classic thing of people swinging machetes and hacking a route through is just pure fantasy.

Sticking to a rigid routine is a crucial part of survival in the jungle. There's no movement allowed before first light or after last light, so you mark those two times of day with a stand-to and a stand-down. In the morning, you get into your wet kit – still damp from the previous day's sweaty march – and observe your arcs of fire. In the evening, you stand down in your wet kit and observe your arcs of fire again. Traditionally, those are the times of day when you're most likely to get attacked: first light and last light. It's when the light is still good enough to mount an assault, but poor enough not to be seen coming. That's the theory behind it, and you do this religiously every day, no matter what.

As soon as it gets properly dark, you get into your dry kit and you turn in. You get a full 12-hours sleep in the jungle, because no one operates at night, but you work twice as hard during the hours of daylight. It's impossible to move at night because it's so dark you can't see, and the foliage is so close it's just pointless trying to do anything other than sleep. You're pretty safe from intruders, because you can hear anybody coming from a way off, and they wouldn't be able to find you because of the lack of light and the denseness of the trees. So, the only sensible thing to do is sleep.

After that initial punishing climb, the first day was spent getting ourselves set up and creating the space where we were going to live. In the jungle you need to be off the ground, to ensure you don't have animals and insects crawling into your sleeping space, so it's essential you construct your 'A-frame' exactly to plan. At the heart of it lies your hammock with a mosquito net around it, with above that a frame of cut branches holding a waterproof cover over you in an inverted V shape – to keep off the rain. In the jungle, your A-frame is your 'safe haven'.

The A-frames start off with just the basics, but before you know it you invariably start to get ambitious, making shelving and then somewhere to sit. They can end up turning into mini-villas. That first night I didn't really manage to get any sleep whatsoever. I'd got god-only-knows-what crawling all over my net, plus there were strange, eerie noises that I'd never heard before echoing through the trees. I'd never imagined such sounds might exist in this world. It normally rains each night for at least a couple of hours, so you'd have the noise of the raindrops beating out a rhythm on your A-frame.

On one level, that first night proved hilarious too, because there were those who hadn't erected their A-frames properly, or they'd used sticks that weren't strong enough. At various points in the night I heard these tremendous cracks of wood breaking in half and the distinctive sound of a body hitting the floor, and then a yell of pain, followed by peals of laughter ringing out through the trees. Repeatedly, there was that distinctive crack, squeal, thump, followed by a giggle for about ten minutes or so.

One of the first key skills we learned was navigation, which is hellish difficult in the jungle, because you can't see any distance. If I'm trekking over a range of hills in Wales and the weather's not down, I can pretty much see my route unfolding before me. I lay out my map, relate the map to the ground ahead, and I can work out exactly where I am and where I need to go. I can read the relief on the map and it becomes relatively easy.

By contrast, in the jungle you're never in a position to do that, because you're enclosed on all sides by a seemingly endless mass of trees. Even if you could see for miles, the relief would look pretty much exactly the same – a never-ending sea of green. In the jungle you have to learn a system called pacing and bearing. You have to rely on counting the paces you've walked, and you have to rely on your compass bearing. If you know that one hundred of your paces equates to one hundred yards walked, then you know you've covered that distance on such and such a compass bearing. You have to stop at every juncture and mark – or make a mental note – of where that leg has taken you to, and then do it all over again. And again and again. It is slow, painstaking and a seriously mind-numbing work.

But as our SAS instructors stressed to us, it's all about learning the basics well. If you don't trust your compass, you're going to end up in serious trouble. If you're covering three or four kilometres in a day, but have your bearing wrong by two or three degrees, at the end of the day that equates to you being a hell of a long way from where you believe you are on your map. Magnify that by several days and it can prove fatal, for obvious reasons. That's why in the jungle, the basics need to be absolutely spot-on all of the time.

As I said, people tend either to love the jungle or hate it. I was one of the former. And because I loved being in the jungle, that took away a lot of the physical challenges for me. In fact, on one level being there reminded me of all those times during my childhood when I'd gone on the run and lived rough in the New Forest. Then, I was living off the land; poaching, scavenging, sleeping under the stars. At times I'd lived on railway sidings in empty huts. But I'd chosen to go on the run, and I'd actually enjoyed the freedom. In truth, I'd loved it, for it was my escape from the kids' homes and the abuse.

Likewise, I thrilled to the sense of freedom and the raw, vibrant riot of life that is the jungle. The sense of being out in the open and living within the constraints of a harsh environment has always bewitched me. Kenya was that in spade-fulls.

On a later jungle exercise with the PWRR (what the Royal Hampshires had amalgamated into) we were set a task designed by one of the Green Army instructors – i.e. not the SAS lads. The aim seemed to be to move us from X-Y-Z in the fastest possible time, so the officers could play at 'ground-manoeuvre formations'. I personally thought it was a waste of all the vital lessons those SAS guys had drilled into us. You didn't conquer the jungle: you had to bend to its constraints and learn to live with it, and to let it do much of the fighting for you. This felt like it was more a rigid test of the competency of the head shed – command – rather than of the skills I was proud to have learned.

I hungered to put our jungle survival skills to use and decided I would conduct my own 'exercise' instead. We'd been split into groups of four, so I turned to my lot – Ade, Paul and Les; all young greenhorns like me – and had a good look to see how they were taking the instructions we'd just been given. They didn't look a great deal happier than I did.

'This exercise looks like a crock of shit, doesn't it?' I ventured

'Yeah to be fair, Phil, it does,' agreed Ade.

'It's not testing us; it's testing the head shed. They're just shunting us about like pawns. Let's do something a little more interesting,' I suggested.

'What d'you mean?' Ade asked.

'Right you lot, watch this,' I announced, by way of answer.

Without further explanation I led our group out of the camp on the bearing we'd been given by the head-shed, before dropping my compass 'accidentally' and then treading on it for good measure.

'Oh dear, I've just managed to drop my compass,' I announced. 'Which direction did they say we walk in? Must be this way. Follow me.'

Deliberately choosing the wrong direction, we trekked into the jungle for a good few hours. Eventually we came to a clear area set under a good high canopy of trees and set up camp. We got our A-frames up, built a fire, caught fish, trapped animals and had a proper jungle experience. For the next four days we did nothing else but enjoy living in the jungle proper, and it was an absolutely brilliant time for all.

At the end of the four days – marking the end-point of the head-shed's exercise – I checked my watch, waiting until it reached a few hours after first light, at which point I fired my two shots into the air. Two hours later, I fired my next two shots, and again we waited.

Not so long after a couple of the SAS instructors appeared out of the middle of nowhere, attracted by the gunfire. 'All right, lads?' they asked us.

'Yeah, yeah, we're fine,' I replied.

We'd had a fabulous time and I was sure the SAS guys knew exactly what we'd been up to – deliberately engineering our own survival exercise. We'd run our own little experiment in jungle living and it was the best four days on the entire trip. We'd put all the skills we'd learned into practice, instead of marching around the jungle, forming up into neat formations, so the commanders could sit back and say: 'Oh, that was a jolly good show, wasn't it?'

Of course, in the future there would come days in the jungle when I just felt like I had no energy left, because we'd been operating for so long at such a high intensity. The jungle can suck the life out of you, but that's also a crucial lesson to assimilate: it's knowing yourself and your kit, learning your limits and accepting that the environment sets the pace.

It was the summer of 1991 when we finished our training in Kenya. Nine years later I would earn my own place in the elite of the British military, and I would find myself back in Kenya once again, training hard so I could fight easy . . . whenever the time might come.

Unbeknownst to any of us, that time was soon to be at hand.

CHAPTER FOUR

FINDING HOME

It was just before my seventeenth birthday when I signed up to join the Royal Hampshires at my local army centre. After all the knockbacks I'd taken through childhood – abandoned, rejected, slung into a string of abusive kids' homes – I finally felt that this might be my chance to wipe the slate clean and start again. I may not have had a family, but perhaps within the British Army I'd find a place that I could call home.

I'd barely completed my first eighteen months training, when I began a tour of Northern Ireland, starting with a two-year stint in Londonderry, initially in a rifle company. During that time I had several close encounters with the IRA, narrowly escaping death twice. Bizarrely, each time I somehow seemed to walk away with a stash of free booze.

The first incident was during a six-week period stationed at the British military base that overlooked the Bogside – the Catholic enclave of Londonderry, Northern Ireland's second city after Belfast. It was in the early hours of the morning when I was woken by a loud explosion coming from the direction of the courthouse, opposite the base. Almost the entire force headed out to take a look, and sure enough just behind the base there was the debris from an explosion.

It wasn't a large bomb, so we suspected that there would very likely be another, much larger secondary device somewhere nearby. This was a typical IRA tactic at the time: detonate one bomb to get everybody's attention, and then when they were gathered together, another bomb to take them all out.

We started to search around the area but we found nothing. By this time, the senior commanders had arrived in their snatch vehicles – lightly-armoured Land Rovers – parking up directly outside a pub called the Gate Bar, a three-storey terraced building. As we knew full well, the Gate Bar was a popular IRA hangout and we'd often see key suspects coming and going. At the end of our daily patrols we'd head down to the Gate Bar, kick over a few stools, eyeball the clientele and check the pub for anything incriminating.

After the bomb blast, I positioned myself outside the Gate Bar, near our snatch Land Rovers. I chatted through the situation with our Sergeant Major, who was also standing guard there. As a parting remark he said to me: 'It ain't over yet, Phil, you mark my words.'

As he set off to cross the road there was this most almighty great explosion. I remember my belly being sucked in as the air was torn from my lungs, and I just knew straight away that the pub had gone up. All around me there was just this huge, swirling, blinding cloud of brick dust, followed by debris falling thick and fast from the sky. I crawled under one of the snatch wagons, which had taken most of the explosion's blast, to shelter from the downpour of rocks and shattered brickwork.

It was impossible to see anything, but I could hear someone

moaning near me, plus screaming and shouting everywhere. Voices were yelling: 'Are you okay? Are you okay?'

It was complete and utter chaos. Miraculously, no one was seriously injured. It turned out that because we'd done the rounds of the Gate Bar, checking the place to death the previous evening, the bombers had been forced to plant their explosive device on the upper floor, rather than at street level. Which was good news for us, as the blast had torn out well above most of our heads. It was fortunate that it had, for otherwise I very likely wouldn't be around to tell the tale today.

When we'd dusted ourselves down, we patrolled what was left of the pub, to see if we could hoover up any clues as to the identity of the perpetrators. A couple of us headed to the pub's cellar, where I seized the opportunity to score us a good few crates of booze. I thought it was the least the Gate Bar could do for us, considering we'd nearly been blasted to death by their unsavoury clientele.

The second occasion on which I had a near-death experience was a few weeks later, when I was assigned to escort duty with one of the ammunition technical officers (ATOs), Chris Smith, a guy who was essentially responsible for bomb disposal. I was like his rifle man cum bodyguard. Everywhere that he went I went too.

It was actually quite a cushy number, because Chris wasn't massively busy at that time, and ATOs on the whole really didn't do that much, unless and until there had been a bombing. So I just sat in his hanger all day, eating toasties, shooting the breeze and playing pool.

But one Friday Chris and I got wind of a bomb that had been placed outside the local RUC police station on the Strand Road.

Sure enough, when we arrived there was a very suspicious looking blue Toyota Hilux van, which was being used as a milk float, but was parked up bang outside the RUC base. It turned out the IRA had hijacked the van, emptied out the milk and replaced it with eight wheelie bins packed with explosives – enough to take out the police station and half of the Strand Road. They'd parked up, set the timers running, and Chris had got the call: you've got an hour before the bombs go off.

I deployed with Chris as his protection, which was fair enough, but it did strike me as being a little messed-up that he got to wear his massive blast suit, helmet, gloves and all the other specialist ATO gear, whereas I was stood there in my bog-standard body armour and with my SA 80 rifle. But needs must, as they say.

Chris got his first visual look at the device and announced: 'Okay, let's send the wheelbarrow down.'

Basically, the 'wheelbarrow' was a remote-controlled robot-ic-gizmo equipped with a 'pigstick' – a device that fires an explosively-propelled jet of water at a bomb to take apart and disrupt its circuitry.

The wheelbarrow trundled down there, triggered the Pigstick and with a sharp crack it hammered into the bomb. But Chris announced that it may have only managed a partial disruption, which meant the bomb was only semi-disabled. With eight wheelie-bins packed full of explosives in there, 'partially-disabled' clearly wasn't going to cut it. Chris sent another robot down, this one equipped with a camera, to check it over more closely.

Once that inspection was done he declared: 'Yeah, happy with that. It's safe. There's nothing going on here.'

Then came the worst part for Chris – having to go and clear everything by hand, up close and personal, just to make absolutely certain there were no nasty surprises. The IRA like nothing better than shooting up or blowing up an ATO, for obvious reasons. These are the guys who mess with their diabolical handiwork. As I was his allocated 'protection', I had to go with him everywhere he went. I could feel myself almost tip-toeing towards the van, knowing full well that the body armour I'd got on would be lucky to stop a bullet, let alone a bomb.

We got to the vehicle and Chris started having a poke round. Deciding it was safe, he started moving the bins off the back of the van and I offered to give him a hand. As I went to grab one of the remaining ones, I moved it slightly and my heart practically stopped: there was another timer, and it had just become visible, strapped to the bottom of the bin. If that triggered, Chris and I would be toast.

I let out a big yell: 'TIMER!'

Chris reacted in a flash, diving onto it and ripping it off. Luckily he managed to dismantle the timer before it could trigger any of the remaining explosives.

Afterwards, when it had all been made absolutely safe, I had a good search through the van. I discovered a whole heap of pound coins fused together with a big lump of melted plastic, in the foot-well of the cab. The day of the intended explosion had evidently been collection day for the milkman doing his rounds. Now, all his takings were melded together with some of the plastic that had melted in the heat of the partial explosion caused by the pigstick. I grabbed the entire lot and took it back with me to our base.

For the next couple of weeks I spent the evenings unsticking, removing and cleaning every single pound coin, until I had amassed a grand sum of £380. A nice little earner, which enabled me to take myself and some of my Royal Hampshire mates on the proverbial piss for several nights running. That was the second time that the IRA had tried to blow me up, and I'd ended up getting a drink on them instead.

After the excitement of those two near-misses, I got word that the battalion's Close Observation Platoon (COP) was recruiting, having recently lost a couple of guys. There was a lot of secrecy surrounding the work the COP did. The guys all seemed to have long scruffy hair and beards – the kind of look that would allow them to blend in on the rougher streets of Derry or Belfast. They were doing lots of extra training – all sorts of stuff that sounded hugely exciting to a nineteen-year-old squaddie like me.

Despite my youth, I stuck my name in the hat with everybody else and was overjoyed to get selected. I headed off to begin training for the COP, which was held in and around the Lydd Ranges, in Kent.

The guys who ran the course, from the chief instructor down, were all highly experienced at the elite end of operations, so this was another peachy opportunity to learn from the best. The COP was a covert reconnaissance unit specially devised for Northern Ireland operations. The course comprised of learning to live rough, to survive on your wits and to gather usable intelligence wherever possible. Those of us selected were told that those were the skills we'd need to use to the maximum, on the kind of operations the

COP got involved in. As a nineteen-year-old regular soldier, that was music to my ears.

I completed the course with flying colours, and needless to say it was brilliant. But one other thing struck me most powerfully: how was it that I could excel in the British military, and even at the elite end of operations, when the British social care system had ground me down into a disillusioned, angry and abused teenager? I'd ended up believing what my abusers had told me: that I was worthless and good-for-nothing; that I was getting exactly what 'my sort' deserved. Here, it wasn't quite a case of zero-to-hero, not yet, anyway. But I was doing well and I felt on top of the world.

Once back in Northern Ireland we got down to some further specialist training. We were dressed in civilian clothing, getting dropped off in unmarked vehicles and using different weapons systems than were the norm. We used to travel across to Ballykinler Army Camp (Abercorn Barracks), on the east coast of Northern Ireland, and do some bespoke training, picking up skills that were well outside the normal run-of-the-mill Royal Hampshire's stuff – like defensive vehicle drills, driving civilian-type cars and vans. Most of all I was getting exposure to highly-experienced and elite operators, which was awesome. In short, I loved every single minute of it.

There was one other major advantage of being in the COP. Because of the secrecy surrounding that one platoon, the rest of my battalion weren't allowed to know exactly what we were up to. You could even steer the commanding officer away from asking too many questions. It was a case of: 'Sorry, sir, I'm not at liberty to talk about any of that.'

The only problem was the jealousy. The green-eyed envy. I was young and I was flying, and that meant there were always people who were trying to trip me up and drop me in the shit. That does seem to be one of life's idiosyncrasies – as soon as you do well, there are those who will try to pull you under, back down to their level.

In a way, this aspect of life in the military did remind me of my time in the children's homes. While in care, if you ever looked like you were pulling ahead, somebody, somewhere, would try to drag you back. Fortunately, those early life experiences had taught me the value of overcoming adversity, even if it meant shutting out all the bad stuff. It can be a doubled-edged weapon, of course, because if you shut out everything forever it can become a problem. But as an immediate survival strategy it does work, and I'd learned to use it to my advantage.

Despite our instructors being tough and unrelenting, and having people sniping from the sidelines, I sailed through the COP training. I'd completed COP selection and was able to join the platoon proper. We went on to do some fantastic edge-of-your-seat operations and I had the time of my life while serving with them.

I remember one job in particular. We had to break into a derelict building above some shops, so that we could keep watch on a doorway in the Bogside – the mainly Catholic neighbourhood which was openly patrolled by the IRA. We were literally living above the shops for quite some time, and had to climb a series of makeshift ladders to get into our hide in the deserted building. We'd get targets allocated to us, along with a file of information about the target and his associates, and then it was our job to come up with a plan – how and when and where we were going to nail him, and what would be the means to do so. We had to do the whole thing ourselves, independently, and I loved the sense of free-thinking and initiative that was involved.

In Londonderry at the time we could still use derelict buildings, towers and the various roof tops to get eyes on a target. For the reconnaissance, I might find myself executing a drive-past in a 'plain-clothes' car – so typically a beaten-up Ford Escort – to take a closer look, or check out places where you might locate yourself in a hide. We were moving one-up, or two-up in vehicles, often around the Bogside, but sometimes into 'the cuds' – the rural areas outside of the city.

We dropped off people from the backs of cars, so they could execute a walk-by recce, and at other times we'd go out riding in the backs of battered old vans. We'd camouflage the vehicles, scuffing them up so that a perfectly smart van or car ended up with a suitably rough and lived-in look to it. When dispatched to check-out remote farms and villages, we'd set up observation posts in woods, bushes, or derelict farm buildings. It was high-risk stuff, as we knew the entire area was an IRA strong-hold.

Although we weren't operating alongside elite forces, we knew the results of our work were being fed directly back to them, to inform active operations. That meant there was a huge onus upon us to ensure that our work was spot on. The more I got involved, the more there came a yearning to want to go out and achieve bigger and better things. Inevitably, during down-time we often found ourselves straying into out-of-bounds areas, just to see if we could pick up extra intel. We would head off for a drink, notifying the guardroom that we'd be going to some safe and friendly location, but instead we'd make a beeline for an area that was altogether more dangerous.

When someone says to you somewhere is out of bounds, you've got to make two assumptions: a) it's the best place in town to seek out the bad guys, or: b) if it's not the best place, it's damn near close to it. For me personally, it was invariably a case of curiosity killed the cat, and it nearly killed Phil Campion on more than one occasion . . .

There was a place on the route down south towards Donegal called the Three-Mile Inn, which was used by both Catholics and Protestants. We used to go there all the time, because invariably it was stacked with women and it was such a great little bar. With us all being in the Close Observation Platoon, mostly we had long hair so we could pass as civvies. We'd drive our local-looking cars there, park up outside and head in for a drink. We'd normally keep one bloke sober, just to keep an eye on things, but other than that we'd take the opportunity to let our hair down, which was often the best way to pick up any stray bits of juicy intel.

Some people knew we were Army, some didn't; others didn't care. For those who did know and did maybe care, when there were two or three of us together they would generally assume we were packing – carrying weapons – and opt to leave well alone. But if you were brazen about it, somebody was bound to get shitty and there were some proper nasty bastards that used to drink there – part of the reason we tended to frequent the place, of course.

Chances were if you made someone shitty, you'd get a breeze

block dropped on your head pretty sharpish. We pushed it close to the line by going there, but it was a great bar and we'd rarely return without having learned something or other of possible import.

One night we headed down to the Three-Mile Inn quite late. We'd been working all day and a couple of car-loads of us made the journey. On one side of the bar was a sort of dance floor and they had this record on by Herbie Hancock, the jazz-fusion-funk artiste. By now I'd downed two or three pints, and for some reason I decided to try a little breakdancing. The locals were loving it. They generally appreciated anyone who was up for a good drink and the craic, and everyone was having a laugh.

After I'd done a few windmills, I pulled this head spin when I suddenly realised I'd forgotten to take my dog tags off before I left camp. This was bad tradecraft, and really bad form on my part. It was a real no-no not to leave your tags behind, especially when operating in the COP. I remember seeing my tags go straight over my nose, spin off my head and slide right across the dance floor, whereupon they came to a halt on the far side of the bar.

Of course, I was the only one on the dancefloor by now, because I was flying around like an idiot doing all sorts of rubbish. People had been watching and clapping and cheering, but it all suddenly stopped when they saw my dog tags go skidding across the floor. The music stopped almost instantaneously, as well. It was one of those *zizzzp* moments, when time sees to stand still. I was thinking to myself: *shit, I'm rumbled and the rest of the lads are in the shit, because everyone knows exactly what dog tags are, no matter which side of the sectarian divide they might be from.*

The atmosphere in the Three-Mile Inn had gone suddenly very icy. There was no avoiding this. No turning a blind eye. I glanced about and fancied I could see some real evil geezers staring at me with an expression that said: *get him*.

I glanced towards my dog tags. If one of the locals picked them up and handed them in, I was in a world of trouble. I had no option but to go and retrieve them. I could feel figures closing in from behind. By the time I reached the tags, all the normal escape routes out of the bar were closed off to me.

Two of my COP mates had seen what had happened and gone straight to the cars, to start the engines and prepare our getaway. Smart thinking. But by the time I reached the tags the only pathway open to me was the toilet, out the back of the bar. As I scooped up the tags and took to my heels, I was sure one of my mates had a fairly good idea that was where I was heading. I hurried towards the gents, my steps getting quicker and quicker, but I could feel a crowd of people surging after me.

I got inside the toilet, kicked the door shut, and booted the bin towards the door before diving into one of the cubicles. I smashed the window out and in a split second I'd got my head and shoulders through, and at exactly that moment the lads came roaring around the back of the pub with the getaway car. But from behind I could hear figures kicking down the door and a voice yelling: 'Brit bastard! It's a fucking Brit.'

I'd wriggled halfway through the window when someone broke down the cubicle door, and I felt them grab hold of my foot. My reaction was to kick him as hard as I could in the chest and the face, repeatedly, trying to drive him off. As I booted my assailant in the head, my COP mates grabbed me by the shoulders and tried to drag me out through the window.

I couldn't afford to leave anything behind, because if I did it was bound to turn up at camp and I'd be in the shit, along with the others. This was deadly serious. It would very likely mean me getting thrown out of the Army, which right then was all that had given me purpose and meaning in life. Under no circumstances whatsoever should we have been here, and we'd even left a false trail back at base, so it was obvious we knew exactly what we were doing.

I knew no matter what, I had to keep hold of my shoe and I was having a right old violent tussle with my chief assailant. I could hear him yelling for others of his comrades to help drag me back in again, the only saving grace being the cubicle, which was too small to allow anymore in. But it was only a matter of seconds now before those in the toilet got wise to this and piled outside, whereupon the shit would really hit the proverbial fan.

Eventually, I gave a final herculean kick with my leg, which connected with something nicely solid and fleshy, and the guy behind gave a yell of pain and released his grip for just a second. In a flash I had my legs through the window and my mates were half-carrying and half-dragging me towards the waiting car. But now there was another problem. Figures had piled out of the pub's rear, and they were moving as if to cut off our escape.

My mates had no choice but to pull their weapons and signal everyone to back the hell off. We jumped into the cars and with a squeal of rubber on gravel, floored the accelerators and headed back towards Derry, as fast as two souped up Ford Escorts could go. On route we managed to get everything packed away and shipshape, before driving back into camp as if nothing untoward had happened. After that episode, I'd learned my lesson: I would always take my dog tags off before I went anywhere covertly.

Not a man amongst us could risk having anything like that on us, when heading into harm's way.

CHAPTER FIVE

SAS SELECTION

After Londonderry with the Royal Hampshires, I did a tour of Fermanagh, and in between I applied for and passed Royal Marines selection. But as no one seemed keen to let me transfer to the Marines, I decided to apply for Para training and succeeded in earning my Para wings, too. I was desperate to move on from the PWRR, so I asked to be transferred to the Parachute Regiment.

My CO went ballistic, claiming that I was being disloyal to my regiment, but I felt I'd served my time. I went back to the COP and continued on operations in Fermanagh, which was when I had the idea that I'd apply for the ultimate instead – SAS selection. My CO was still unwilling to let me go, and appeared determined to get his pound of flesh. But eventually he partially relented and we cut a deal.

I would have to become a patrol commander in his Close Observation Platoon (COP) and serve my time with them on our next posting, to Omagh. If I made a decent job of that, then he would let me put myself forward for SAS selection. So that is exactly what I proceeded to do.

People often ask what the secret is to succeeding at selection. For sure, it was a question I pondered too, back in the day. Most often, you'd end up talking to the blokes who had failed, and rarely to those who had passed. The reasons why are self-evident. Those who have passed are busy serving in the SAS and are sworn to secrecy. Those who haven't made it aren't constrained in the same ways. There's a world of difference in the advice you will be offered. The bloke who's failed will tell you how nigh-on impossible selection is, stressing the practical, hands-on and extreme physical challenges.

The bloke who's passed will invariably say: 'It isn't so bad, you've just got to stick your mind in. It's all in the head.'

I knew a couple of guys serving in the SAS at the time and their advice proved invaluable. 'Don't go mad and don't over-train,' they told me. They added that when I did train, I should aim to develop my mental toughness at least as much as the physical side.

Too many candidates turn up having done far too much training, and they just break themselves in the first couple of days. They're basically exhausted before they even get started. I didn't want to be one of those who had to bail out because of an injury, when it could all have been avoided by not training like a madman in the first place.

Towards the end of my time in Northern Ireland, the cease-fire was in place, which meant I was able to dedicate as much of my spare time to preparing for selection as I wanted. We had a swimming pool on camp and I got permission to go in with my combats and webbing on, if I wanted. Often, I'd dive in with all my clothes on, and sometimes all my gear, boots included – so a good extra two kilos or more. It was tiring and irksome labouring up and down the pool dressed like that, but it wasn't stressing my joints, and most importantly it was for real. If I had to swim during selection, it wouldn't be in my Speedos on the Cote d'Azur, that was for sure.

There were three of us from my unit who were getting ourselves ready. We got permission to travel to the Mourne Mountains, which lie some fifty miles south of Belfast, in County Down, near the border with the Irish Republic. The highest, Slieve Donard, at 2790 feet, is just a little short of Pen y Fan, the highest peak in Wales, which forms part of the Brecon Beacons, where selection takes place for real. Like the Brecons, the Mourne Mountains are a mass of sweeping hump-backed folds of wild greys and greens, wherein the weather is eternally unpredictable, and you often experience all four seasons in one day. They say you know it's going to rain there if you haven't had a storm for the last couple of hours.

It was perfect terrain in which to train and to get some proper hill walking done, which is essential to getting yourself properly conditioned, and to building what we term 'mountain legs'. What you don't need to do is *hill running*, especially with a massive pack on your back, because you're going to get plenty of opportunities to prove yourself on selection, and you need to preserve your energy and avoid injury.

Most days we'd walk and walk and walk, from first to last light. After several weeks in the Mourne Mountains I was feeling good. But I hadn't yet tested myself in proper man-territory as it were – on the Brecons themselves, where the rubber would truly hit the road.

With a few months to go before selection – which I'd be attempting in the first week of January – we got permission to head to Wales, to do some training on the Brecons. We couldn't afford to pay for any accommodation, so one of the lads persuaded the staff at what was then Cwrt y Gollen Military Training Camp, to let us camp out in the cricket pavilion, near the town of Crickhowell.

For three weeks we went up into the Brecons each and every day and just walked and walked the hills. We tried as much as possible to ape the routes we knew we would have to cover on selection. Some might say that's bordering on cheating. But knowing what I know now, it was the best thing we could have done to get ourselves ready. As those SAS instructors had told me, years back, in Kenya – *train hard, fight easy*. Well, we were training hard *and smart*, so as to make it a little easier on ourselves when we were tested to the limits.

We did all the various routes – the Fan Dance, VW Valley, Point 264 – learning to adapt to the individual nuances and idiosyncrasies of each. Some of the slopes were massively steep and a true test of physical stamina and mental grit. Other areas, although less hilly, consisted of mile after endless mile of these hideous mounds of tufted grass, set within a marshy-type terrain, which meant you could never really get a proper foothold. We termed those areas 'babies heads,' because of the physical resemblance of those rounded tufts of grass to a young infant's head. The ground was so soft and shitty underfoot that you could literally take two or three paces forwards, five sideways and one left, plus one up and one down, just to move an inch or two forward. Alongside all the hill walking, we added in a bit of swimming and gym work, which helped to increase our overall strength and fitness, without stressing our joints.

We did proper timed test runs too, concentrating on some of the key routes – like the famous Fan Dance. As we'd been briefed in detail about what was going to happen to us on selection proper, we decided to follow it to the letter. The Fan Dance is a fifteen-mile run, one of the more well-known tests of SAS selection, and it starts at a place known by the pub that is located there, the Storey Arms. The pub sits at the bottom of a steep ascent (886 metres), which is the punishing and brutal incline of the Pen y Fan itself. Although this was only a rehearsal, we knew it would be as much a test of mental strength as it would be of physical stamina and fitness.

Somehow, we had to keep reminding ourselves that when we did this for real, we'll be chasing the clock, and would be hounded by the directing staff (DS) – those who run selection – and that it would be utterly relentless. You're supposed to keep tabbing at about four kilometres an hour to complete the Fan Dance in time, but we had been told you're never given enough time, so you'd have to learn to judge it the best you could. Ultimately, the Fan Dance requires you to come in on the heels of the DS. If you lose them or fail to keep up, you're binned.

For our rehearsals, we'd carry a 40-pound Bergen on our backs, just as we would do for real. We had been told that if it was found to be even slightly under-weight, the DS would just go to the side of the road, pick up one of the biggest rocks they could find and stick that in your Bergen instead. So while you may have been two pounds under at the start, you'd be ten 10 pounds over for the rest of the course.

We were told there'd likely to be a big old squad on the day of the race – about 30 or 40 of us, who'd all be going at it neck-and-neck to keep at the front. Like with any race, there was the chance that everyone would try to bunch up at the start, and once the DS got going, being left at the back could be the deciding factor between a pass or a fail. We knew it would be everyone for themselves, so there would be no waiting for anyone and no one would be cut the slightest slack. It would be a case of lead, follow or get out the bastard way.

The three of us set off up the side of the Fan laden down with our Bergens. It's steep and we knew we were going to have to set a good pace to stay on top of things. Once we crested the top we tore across Corn Du and then down Jacob's Ladder, and hit what's called the Sheep Track or the Roman Road, which leads to a turnaround point at the reservoir at Torpantau.

We knew when we did this for real there would be several checkpoints along the way, where you'd be made to stop, remove your Bergen and grab your water bottle and take a drink. You'd then be made to show the DS your map, point out your present location and indicate where the next checkpoint was and your intended route to get there. No one offered you the slightest help or advice. If your navigation is shit, you're utterly on your own and you will fail.

As we three steamed along the Roman Road, we could only imagine what it would be like with over ten times our number competing to be the first of the pack. It'd be pure carnage. All the more reason to get ahead at the very start and to stay ahead. We hit the turnaround point at Torpantau reservoir and began to retrace our steps.

On the way back, the view is daunting, because you can see all the way down this die-straight Roman Road for miles and miles, at the far end of which you can see Jacob's Ladder, rising in the distance like some impossible apparition.

There is a reason it's got an evil reputation up there on the Fan – you just know you're going to hurt like crazy going up the Ladder. All the while we knew this would be as much of a mental challenge as it is a physical. People have been known to drop out simply because they lose sight of the DS. That doesn't mean it's all over: it certainly doesn't mean you're doomed to fail. But people get all strung out and think they've had it and decide to VW-- making a voluntary withdrawal. But if the kind of childhood I had has taught me anything, it's to keep going no matter what and to never, ever give up. I might fail the course, but I'm sure as hell not going to give in and fail myself. At the end of the day I'd rather come in running as hard as I can with a smile on my face, and be failed by the DS, than voluntarily walk off the hill because I failed myself in my own head.

The three of us reach the stage where we are halfway up Jacob's Ladder. It's a ridiculous hill – a proper killer – and it just breaks you getting up it. We might have been in a test run but we were giving it all we had. I got a second wind and started going for it with renewed vigour. I powered up the ladder, got across the top of the fan and I literally began to run as hard as I could down the far side. I knew there wasn't the slightest incline ahead of us now, or at least nothing that could touch the pain and angst of Jacob's Ladder.

In my mind, I could fly up anything and I'm running like the wind. As I skip down the side of the Fan, my attitude towards selection crystallized in my mind. I wanted to go in pushing it to the max every single time. That way, if I didn't pass, at least I wasn't going to end up walking off the hill, head bowed in abject defeat, or having to be carried off by someone.

As I came around the last bend, and the Storey Arms hoved into view, in my mind's eye I knew exactly what I was going to do. I was going to make it, come hell or high water. This was my chance to prove all the nay-sayers and the gropers and the abusers in the kids' home plain wrong: I was not a worthless piece of crap and I could and I would compete with the best.

December arrived, and my Royal Hampshires battalion (now renamed the PWRR) was about to get its next posting – away from Northern Ireland, to Tidworth Camp, a military training base set in leafy Wiltshire. For some reason the only accommodation they could find for me was in the barracks in Bulford, just a few miles down the road on Salisbury Plain.

Work was quiet and with few duties to attend to, I took some leave that I had owing. With a month to go before SAS selection, I suddenly realise that I'd lost quite a bit of weight with all the training. Once I head for the Brecons and it all began for real, I just know the kilos would start falling off me. I needed to start eating and to rest, so as to build up some reserves.

When you are on selection, you can eat almost anything you want because you are burning up so many calories. You can have double cooked breakfast with all the extras, all the burgers you can get down you for lunch, and as much pizza and Coke as you can manage that evening. You can also drink a good few of pints on top of that lot as well.

I decided I needed a bit of that right then. I was going to take December nice and easy, and so for the next few weeks I just ate, drank and was really quite merry. Knowing that I was possibly going to lose as much as two or three stone while on the selection, I wolfed down mega-portions of fish-and-chips, drank Guinness by the bucketful, and I actually managed to put back on some of the weight.

In those days, I wasn't that bulked up, at only fourteen stone. Considering it was more than likely I'd come off the course weighing only about eleven stone, I figured putting a bit of beef on beforehand would hold me in good stead. I kept myself ticking over fitness-wise by running a few of the back tracks around Bulford and swimming, but December was my month on the beer really, and I didn't deviate from that plan.

It was at this time that I took my car off the road, because my mate was going to pick me up and take me to Wales to start selection, so it was a way to save a bit of money. The day before we were supposed to be driving up there together, I got a phone call from him from out of the blue, telling me he'd had a change of heart. He wasn't going anymore. This was on the Sunday, with selection proper starting on the Monday. In those days you couldn't just tax your car online. Mine was insured and it was MOT'd, but there was no tax disc on it because I'd taken it off the road.

I decided it was shit or bust time. I'd have to take a gamble and drive down to Sennybridge, from where selection started, and deal with the tax disk issue whenever I got a spare moment. After all, what other option was there in the time available? I could hardly call Mummy and Daddy to ask them for a lift. I don't exactly have any. And at such short notice all my Army mates were on duties, so none of them were free.

I fired up the Ford Escort, got behind the wheel and slipped out of camp, hoping to keep a low profile. Murphy's law is in play, however: *if it can go wrong it will.* On my way out of the camp gates I got pulled over by a copper. It couldn't get any worse, especially as this guy was one of those total rules-obsessed, by-the-book types. He'd noticed that I didn't have a tax disc showing in my windscreen, and no matter what I might have said about being on a mission, and where I was driving to and why, he was having none of it.

'No, no, no, lad,' he shook his head, dismissively. 'It doesn't matter where you're going or why, you need to have a tax disc. That's the law.'

He issued me with a 'producer', meaning that I had to present my documents at a nominated police station within the next few days. In the back of my mind I was thinking – *I can't do that, because I'm just about to start selection. If I don't show up with the documents, I'll get a court summons, which will be even worse. How do I know I'll even be able to get to court?* It seems as if my attempt at selection is cursed somehow, and before I've even got started.

Sure enough, I got the court summons. I couldn't tell my parent regiment that I was up for a court appearance, for obvious reasons, so I claimed that I had an urgent hospital appointment come through at short notice. I got granted time out to make the 'appointment', but I would need to be driven there and back, so I can keep up with the relentless pace of things. I got allocated a military driver, to make sure I made it on time.

On the day of my court appearance, I sat with my military driver as he speeds me towards what he believed was an urgent hospital appointment, wondering what the hell I was to tell him. Eventually, I decided there's no option but to come clean. I confessed that rather than him delivering me to hospital, he was actually going to have to drive me to a court hearing.

He threw me a disbelieving look. 'Oh, for fuck's sake –'

'Listen, don't worry about it,' I cut in, trying to make light of it. 'Just come in and watch the show.'

'What are you up for?' he demands. 'And have you at least got a solicitor?'

'Not having a tax disc. Yeah, and I'm representing myself.'

I can't exactly say he looked impressed. But we were almost there, so little sense in turning back.

I lodged my plea in the court, which was 'not guilty', of course. The regulations weren't the same back then, and I've decided to argue that I did have a tax disc, just that it wasn't on display. I got cross-examined and then, because I represented myself, I got to cross-examine the policeman.

I started with all the normal stuff – what's your name, position within the police, that kind of thing. Despite my predicament, a part of me started to enjoy myself. I began to pace the court room like Hercule Poirot, firing questions at this policeman – it sure made a change from being on the other side of things, which was how I'd spent much of my troubled youth, of course. More to the point, I'd noticed that the guy who'd driven me down here was watching closely from the gallery, and he seemed to be enjoying himself mightily. In fact, he was grinning ear to ear.

Eventually, I popped the million-dollar question: 'So, why exactly did you stop me? What led you to stop my car?'

'Simple. I couldn't see a tax disc in the windscreen.'

'Well there you go. Just like I was saying – it wasn't in the windscreen, it was on the dashboard. I told you that I had a tax disc at the time, but that it wasn't on display, but still you've dragged me into court for not having one.'

It was then that the judge intervened: 'Is that true?' he demanded of the copper. 'Why didn't you check? Why didn't you check what he'd told you?'

The policeman seemed properly lost for words. I repeated that my tax disc holder hadn't been positioned properly, that was all. Somehow, I managed to get away with it.

But as I was making my way out of the court, case-dismissed, I practically had a heart attack. The last person I ever wanted to see was standing on the court steps just a few feet away from me. It was my commanding officer from the 2nd Battalion of the PWRR – Colonel Newton. In an effort to avoid him seeing me coming out of the court, I slide around the other way, so I could act as if I was just casually passing by.

I braced myself and launched into the fray. 'Hello sir, how are you?' I announced, acting all surprised to see him there.

'Corporal Campion, what are you doing here?' replied my CO, who looked genuinely nonplussed.

'Yeah, I've got a weekend off. I'm just doing some shopping.' Desperate to avoid any further questions – like why are you at the courthouse then? – I made out that I was really busy. 'Yeah,

yeah, got to go. Yeah, yeah, nice one sir. See you back at camp when I'm done.'

At a safe distance I reconnected with my military driver. He'd watched me represent myself in court – firing questions at the policeman as I marched to and fro, with my little notebook in hand – after which I've managed to give my own CO the slip. A part of him has warmed to the performance. You have to be a self-starter in the SAS and to be able to think on your feet. You need to be independently-minded and a lateral-thinker, not to mention something of a maverick. You have to be willing to expect the unexpected, and to be ready for it whenever it might hit you.

He figured I had just demonstrated a good dose of those kind of qualities in that court room.

CHAPTER SIX

THE CIRCUIT

I spent a dozen years serving in the British military, which was the absolute saving of me – after the kind of start I'd had at the hands of the British care system. The military taught me many, many things: self-discipline, self-belief, principles. Crucially, my time serving imbued within me a sense of self-value and self-worth, which my experiences during my first seventeen years of life had done everything to tear apart and destroy.

It had also taught me the vital lesson of a classless society. Not rank-less – but classless, in the sense that we are all created equal. Taking that on-board wholeheartedly, I fervently believed I was as good as any man, no matter that I had grown up in a council house. After all, your family background, your schooling, your pedigree and your wealth are irrelevant – bullets do not discriminate on such grounds, and we are all equal on the level playing field of the battleground.

Upon leaving the military I decided to seize the bull by the proverbial horns, and to seek work on the private military circuit – turning my elite forces skills to protecting people and assets in some of the more conflict-torn areas of the world. That was how I found myself landing a job in Togo, a tiny West African nation with a population of only eight million people, wedged between Ghana, Benin and Burkina Faso.

Like much of West Africa, you should never expect a red carpet. Crime and corruption very often go hand in hand, and Togo is no exception. But where the country really excels is with its horrendous human rights record, for which it's earned itself something of an unrivalled reputation.

According to reports from charities like Amnesty International and the US government's State Department, the country's security forces regularly carry out arbitrary arrest, beatings with rifle butts, batons and belts, and horrific detention. They have a habit of dragging detainees out of their police cells, and subjecting them to mock executions. Prison conditions are harsh to the point of being life-threatening, with excessive force – including torture – being used regularly, resulting in injury or death. In other words, if you get on the wrong side of the 'law' in Togo you are seriously in the proverbial.

A good friend of mine had recommended me to a guy I shall call Julian Smith, who was running a private security company based in London, called Zero-Risk Security. Julian telephoned me to say he'd got a job starting off in Togo, escorting an oil tanker from there to Nigeria, safeguarding it from piracy and any other such shenanigans. Would I like to come to his offices to have a chat about it, he asked. I was totally up for a bit of anti-piracy work, so I caught the next train to London.

Piracy around West Africa is rife and at least half a dozen ships are attacked by these desperadoes of the high seas every year. I would have more than my fair share of anti-piracy work over the years, devising cunning plans to defeat the ocean bandits. In my time I'd create such deterrents as the 'bouncing barrel' – empty metal oil drums suspended over the side of the ship on ropes, so that they that bounce up and down on the ocean waves, knocking out even the most hardened pirate who might try to clamber aboard. That would be one of my brainwaves, plus the ultimate in the spur-of-the-moment missiles: a ship's commercial refrigerator launched over the side, perfect for sinking a boat-load of gun-toting hijackers. It was an area I would get to know better than most, but Togo was to be one of my first shots at this anti-piracy lark.

I arrive at Julian's offices in a little back street near Victoria Station, where he proceeds to brief me on the job. It all sounds fine, until he mentions that he wants me to fly out with several sets of body armour and helmets, to equip me and the rest of the crew on the ship.

The minute I hear those words, the scepticism kicks in: 'Whoa, whoa, whoa . . . body armour? In that part of the world they tend to go ape-shit if you're travelling with anything ballistic-related, or connected to security.'

By way of answer Julian hands me the paperwork for the body-armour. 'No, no, mate, it's fine,' he reassures me. 'Take a look. I've got all the documentation squared away.'

I do as he's suggested and it does all seem to be utterly authentic. The papers are signed off by, and even have the stamp of, the Togo-lese embassy. I can't really ask for more, and can't see any reason to argue. Forty-eight hours later I catch a flight from London to Lomé–Tokoin airport, in Togo. With a couple of stops en route, I'm there in just over eleven hours, arriving in the cool of the early morning. As we come into land, it's all palm trees and white beaches, enshrouded in a dawn sea-mist. In fact, it looks distinctly paradisiacal.

The arrangement is that I will meet a team of locals who are based on the ship, in the port of Lomé, just a short drive from the airport. I'll bring the body armour and helmets with me, while they will supply the weapons we'll need once we hit the open seas.

The airport is small but quite modern by African standards. As I stand in line waiting at the luggage carousel it all seems perfectly pleasant and unthreatening. The two big black holdalls, one containing four sets of body armour and the other four helmets, plop out of the conveyor belt and I reach forward to pick them up. I pass through the security checkpoint, putting the bags through the scanner, and wait for them to come out on the other end. No one gives the slightest sign there is any problem, and I figure I am good to go.

I turn to leave, but notice there is one last X-ray machine, right before the exit. I try my best to casually swerve around it, after which I continue striding confidently towards the exit, but to my right I hear a loud male voice cry out: 'No, no, no, sir. You must come through here!'

I turn to see five uniformed airport officials gathered around the x-ray machine, eyeing me with more than a little attitude. I try flashing my biggest smile and say: 'Yeah, of course, no problem. Sorry, didn't see you guys.'

I hand one of the security geezers the bags and he feeds them into the machine. I'm still smiling, but I've got one eye on the face of the guy who's gazing into the screen, which will reveal exactly what's inside my holdalls. As I watch him, I tell myself: *You guys aren't going to be happy with this, are you . . .*

The first bag appears on the screen and his face changes in an instant. But bizarrely, it isn't the reaction of someone getting antsy; it's almost as if he's ecstatic at what he's seeing. It looks as if I've just made his day. Both bags go through, and both get hauled off. The officials muster, smelling their prey. Not a word is said to me as one of them clomps off into a nearby office, but I can sense the storm clouds of Togo officialdom gathering thick and fast. There's still not been a word been offered by way of explanation as to why I've been waylaid, but I can hazard a good guess.

I stand there for ages, while people are coming and going all around. Gradually, a whole mish-mash of airport officials appear. It's like a lucky dip of uniforms, with one figure arriving after another and all of them dripping in ridiculous amounts of gold braid. It's pretty clear there's going to be a big deal made out of what's in my bags, yet so far no one has told me diddly-squat. It's a typical case of 'TIA' – This Is Africa, as we used to call it in the business.

While they're making me wait – and sweat, for I presume that's their intention – I'm not saying a word to anyone. There really is no point. I am keeping my mouth shut at this stage of the campaign. It's at times like this when I think back to my days in the military and reflect on what I learned. The most dangerous part of being captured is at the stage when you first get taken, because that's when you tend to encounter people with the least discipline. As you move further up the chain, there's a greater chance that people are saddled with a higher degree of responsibility, and might actually be tasked to keep you alive. But consequently, they are far less inclined to let you escape. That's why you have it drilled into you to escape at the earliest opportunity.

Conversely, when you actually get rumbled, caught or lifted, that's the most dangerous time, because you're with people who don't know anything about you, who may well be scared, and who are most likely to beat you up, or even shoot you. But again, they're less likely to be vigilant or to stop you from breaking free. Strictly speaking, I haven't been captured yet. No one has held a gun to my head or clapped me in chains. But somehow, I'm in no doubt that I am not permitted to go anywhere.

Eventually this guy in a suit comes ambling over. He speaks decent English and he explains that he wants me to open my bags. I unzip the two black holdalls. By now there are a dozen uniformed officials standing around, and they look as if they're getting seriously excited. I drag out the first set of body armour and helmets, and there is an audible gasp. They stand there gawping and giving it all the shock, horror and awe act, as if I'd just produced a human head.

The man in the suit turns to eye me: 'So, are you a military man, yes?'

'No, no, no,' I reassure him. 'I'm just here delivering this stuff. Plus I've got all the paperwork.' I take out the official documentation and hand it to him. 'Here, take a look.'

He accepts the paperwork, but just stares at me blankly, without bothering to so much as glance at the documents. Waving them at me, he says: 'What is this? What is this?'

I do my best to explain, but I know I am on a losing wicket. It's plain as day that he's not interested in any official approvals, not even if they've been signed off by God Almighty himself. He's already made up his mind about me, and I'm going to get lifted come what may. Finally, he wanders off to talk to another official, and again without offering the slightest explanation. I know what this is about. It's all about demonstrating who has the power here, and who, by contrast, has zero power.

Countless hands rustle through the bags. They drag out everything and anything they can, piling the contents on the table. They're like a bunch of magpies eyeing up anything shiny they can lay their hands on. I see my Leatherman multi-tool and my first aid kit being passed around. Knowing what I do about Togo's record of arbitrary arrest and torture, I figure they'll be experts at dreaming up some particularly twisted and painful procedures, and with the multi-tool the options must be endless.

In my mind, I'm going through the Leatherman's repertoire. The needle-nose pliers – ideal for tight spaces and manipulating small, delicate items, like tonsils, fingernails or testicles. Like-wise, they could cause havoc with the rough-cut saw, and with the various different blades and screwdrivers. Then there's the corkscrew – perfect for winding into a torture victim's eyeball.

They put the shiny kit down and one of them picks up one of the helmets and places it on his head. The others follow suit, and before long there are Togolese airport officials to left and right dressed in various combinations of Kevlar helmets and body armour. It's a right old clown-show, but oddly enough I fail to find it very amusing. That's because there is a distinctly sinister undertone.

When they tire of that, they bung all my stuff back into the bags and several of them escort me into the nearest office. The guy in the suit tells me to sit down and they start 'umming' and 'ahing' amongst themselves.

Finally he pops the question: 'So, you are a mercenary? You are coming here to cause trouble? You are coming to Togo to fight? Are you a fighting man?'

Either they honestly suspect that I'm a gun for hire, or they're building a case in an effort to scare the living daylights out of me, so as to extract the biggest possible bribe. I still favour the latter explanation. I try to be polite and helpful, while not really answering any of their questions directly. In my mind I'm weighing things up. Yes, Togo officials have a nasty reputation for beating the crap out of anyone they detain and they don't hesitate to resort to torture. But right now I'm being held at the airport. I'm still in the early phase of capture, if it is that, and it's best to say as little as I can for as long as possible.

Fairly abruptly, the guy in the suit changes tact. 'You are not answering me. But I warn you, if you are a mercenary, you will very likely be executed. Do you want to be executed? No. So answer my questions. Are you a military man? Do you come to Togo to fight?'

My mind is racing now. I start to worry that if I say the wrong thing, it could prove terminal. This may no longer be about simple bribes. Men in suits tend to be intelligence types – spooks – and they generally get called in if a serious threat is suspected – like a bunch of white mercenaries flying in to topple the Togolese government. There have been internationally-backed military coups before in this country, so the concept has substance and precedent.

Either way, being threatened with execution upon arrival at Togolese airport is certainly not the kind of jaunt that Julian sold to me, back in London. The guy in the suit seems to have reached some kind of verdict. He turns to his fellow officials: 'I have many more questions for this man. We need to detain him.'

A separate force of uniformed guys pile in. The man in the suit tells me these are airport police, but of course you never know quite what you're getting here in Africa. They bundle me into the back of a van with no windows, and that's when I start to truly switch on, preparing myself mentally and physically for what might be coming. Thankfully, the British military are some of the best at conduct-after-capture training, which is specifically designed to simulate the kind of things you'll face when taken prisoner by the bad guys. I run through in my mind all that I was taught, so as to ready myself for whatever lies ahead.

It's not a long trip in the van, less than ten minutes, and I can't see anything in terms of where we're going, but still I figure I've been removed from the airport, which is significant. In any capture or imprisonment scenario, there's always a progression in events, and knowing the appropriate action and response at each level is vital. While I was at the airport, things were at Level One. Now I've been removed from there – most likely to a holding area or police station – they're at Level Two. Level Three will be if and when they move me to a prison-type compound, which will mean I am really in the shit, because the further down the line you go the harder it is to escape.

The van door opens and they bundle me out. It looks as if we've reached some kind of a police station, but I don't get taken inside. Instead, lying directly adjacent to the station building is this shipping container. It's your typical 10 x 8-foot steel box-type contraption, and it's being baked in the mid-morning African sun. One of the police guys opens the door and propels me inside, before closing and locking the door behind him. It cranks shut with that ominous, creaking, penned-in sound shipping containers always seem to conjure up.

Now, I hate being locked up. I hate even more being locked up in small, dark claustrophobic spaces, ones in which countless other individuals have suffered horribly. I presume it's obvious why. As a kid, I got locked inside places which were rife with beatings and abuse. So to be locked up equates to fear and terror and, increasingly, to impending perversions. To be incarcerated in a place such as this, in a country such as this, by a group of this type of people, while accused of being a mercenary – well, it doesn't get a whole lot worse.

It's pitch-black inside, and it's already suffocatingly hot, though it's not yet even midday. Plus . . . it stinks. As my eyes gradually adjust to the gloom, I can see the one source of light: they've cut a tiny, crude hole in the front of the container at floor level, about the size of my palm. I kneel down and get my cheek right up close to the stinking floor, so I can sneak a look outside. I don't doubt there is urine, faeces and blood on the floor, judging by its stickiness, let alone other unmentionables. I don't fancy inspecting things too closely, but I'm forced to crouch down on my hands and knees, in an effort just to get some air.

I console myself with the thought that at least I won't die of oxygen deprivation. The downside is this: the hole is at the perfect height for any of the kids that seem to be hanging around outside to piss through. Which may help explain the smell in here. It reeks, and as the heat builds through the day it must end up cooking whatever poor bastard is locked inside.

From what I can see via the hole, the police station seems to lie at the end of a dirt track. I see people milling about and the kids playing football. The rear of the shipping container is in total darkness and I don't even want to check out what might be lying back there, decomposing amidst the heat and stench and the flies. Already, it feels like an airless oven. I check my watch by the light coming in through the hole. It's still only 10.30 hours local time. It will get hotter and hotter as the sun beats down, until yours truly gets fried alive.

While the security guards confiscated the bags with the body armour and helmets, bizarrely they have left me with my hand luggage. It's a times like this that you have to be thankful for small mercies. At this stage, I haven't yet been searched properly, which is to my advantage. I do an inventory of my kit, and luckily I still have my satellite phone on me, which was stuffed in my hand luggage. Unbelievable.

That phone is my trump card, but first I have to figure out exactly how best to use it. I have limited battery power, no means of recharging it, and at any time they might return to search me properly. I have to presume I can make a very limited number of calls, so they have to be to the right people for all the right reasons.

I squat down and try to think things through. I attempt to apply some reason and hard logic to an utterly unreasonable and unpredictable situation, to see the best way through. Despite the immediate threat of execution, Africa is one of those continents where bribery is a way of life. Most officials are willing to turn a blind eye, in return for a nice little back-hander. It's more than likely that this whole song-and-dance is designed to soften me up, so once the bribe is asked for, the captive – or his employer – is only too happy to pay it.

At this moment, when everything appears to have gone seriously to rat-shit, I will need to bank upon the immorality of the Togolese officials. But I'm also aware that people this way down the chain of command are often incapable of thinking their actions through properly. On a whim, they could at any time chain me up and give me an OBE – one behind the ear – in other words, a bullet in the head.

There is another possible scenario, which I force myself to consider. They could be viewing me as a valuable commodity, to be flogged to some nasty Islamist faction. Across West Africa there are scores of Islamist extremist groups, and you're never more than a car-journey away from some pretty unpleasant people, where a hostage like me trussed up in an orange jump suit would have a serious price on his head. I have a good idea of the kind of ransom I might be worth. I'm former British military, elite forces. That alone would make me one a hell of a trophy for the likes of al-Qaeda.

I consider my options. I have nothing suitable on my person with which to bribe the Togolese police and security officials. I wasn't carrying a great deal of cash. I didn't think I'd have need of it, because you can't exactly spend much on the high seas. The one thing I do have is my phone. My only hope is to use it to call some people who can hopefully offer to transfer some serious money across to my captors.

I kneel in the putrid mess on the floor, and I manage to poke my satphone's stubby aerial through the palm-sized hole, and somehow I get a signal. I phone the offices of Zero-Risk Security. They organised this trip and they swore blind the papers would get me through. They should have every reason to want to get me out of all this. A woman answers. It's the secretary. She sounds about as uninterested in my predicament as it is possible to get, and there's no one else in the office. I finally get her to agree to make some calls and to get those who can look into it.

But frankly, I don't hold out any great hopes of deliverance from their end any time soon.

CHAPTER SEVEN

ROASTED

After about an hour, a guard arrives to question me. While I've kept my mouth shut at the airport, the situation has now changed markedly. I know it's to my advantage to try to build some rapport with those holding me. I need to get them to see me as a fellow human being, not just as a faceless prisoner. More to the point, I've done absolutely nothing wrong, so I am the innocent party. But I want to try to encourage some kind of friendly interaction, so for now I need to avoid all hostility.

The first thing the guy does is search my kit and sure enough he finds my Sat phone. I have to try to take advantage of this. I tell him I've wanted to get the phone into their hands ever since being locked up, but had no way to communicate with anyone. I ask him to use it to make some calls, and to speak to whoever he needs to in order to open up negotiations. Whether that's the chief of police, or their minister of the interior or of Security, we need to get a conversation going over the terms for my release.

The message seems to hit home. I watch him leave and hear the door creak shut behind, and shortly after a group of police-types gather outside, clustered around my Sat phone. I hear them make their first calls. It strikes me as the ultimate irony that here I am being detained, while those holding me begin negotiations for my release using my own bloody phone. But I reason that the more calls I can get them to make on my behalf, the more people will know that I'm here and will be able to testify if I do get an early OBE. If they do think about slotting me, at least they might realise they'll get in trouble for it afterwards.

I start to chat with the guards and talk about football – the universal language of humankind. I know if I continue to stay completely shtum, I'm going to put their backs up and turn them against me. As it stands, they could potentially hold me here for days without agreeing anything with anybody. It's down to me to turn this situation around, by being as cooperative as possible and by basically talking my way out of here.

It's at times like this that I force myself to think of the upside – that the situation could actually be a whole lot worse. All right, I'm in a bit of a bind. I'm locked in a roasting metal box in Africa, being cooked like the proverbial Christmas turkey, with people around me insisting I'm about to face imminent execution. Even so, my immediate thoughts at this stage of proceedings are that actually, I'm quite fortunate, because they haven't beaten me up yet. Yes, it's hot and stinking, but I'm still physically intact, all my teeth are in my head and my limbs and internal organs are all present and correct.

It's around midday when the door of the shipping container creaks open and they drag me out and frog-march me into the police station. It's now that they start the serious business of interrogating me about what it is that I'm doing in their country. Why did I come here with these military things? Where are my guns?

Who am I meeting? What are we planning? The interrogation is relentless and I'm starting to fear that things are spiralling out of control. Somehow, I can't see me getting out of here any time soon.

During the interrogation, there are the typical types of questioning I've come to expect. There's the straight yelling and bawling, which is designed simply to frighten. There's the repetitive type of questioning, designed to wear you down, and there's the type of questioning where people are seemingly being very nice to you. It's psychologically proven that unless you are actively guarding against it, we naturally tend to open up to the nice guy – the person who appears to be on our side.

I remind myself to be on guard for this. I try to remain friendly, providing minimal, but respectful answers to their questions. At the same time I keep encouraging them to speak to the London office of Zero-Risk Security, so that this can all be sorted out amicably. It doesn't feel particularly amicable by the time the interrogation is done, and I fear that much more of this and it's going to turn very physical, and distinctly nasty.

I'm dragged back to the shipping container, where I'm left for several more hours. Locked there in the dark, the heat and the suffocating stink keep rising by the second. I'm sweating like the proverbial glass-blower's arse. Physically, I can feel myself beginning to go downhill. I'm seriously worried that I'm going to fry alive in this metal container, it's so baking-hot. I've had no access to water or any other drink for hours, and my mouth's as dry as the Sahara. It won't be long before my body starts closing down.

Dehydration sets in when any human being suffers a deficit in the normal levels of body-water. Water accounts for around 70 per cent of our body weight, and it is essential for just about every human function. The fact I've had no water for several hours, combined with the fact I'm dripping in sweat, means I'm losing valuable fluids and salts by the second.

It only takes as little as one per cent dehydration for symptoms to start to kick in, and they quickly begin to affect your body and your mind. In the earliest stages, you start to feel lethargic and have headaches and your memory and attention become impaired. If the water doesn't get replaced, your motor coordination is affected, with your muscles feeling weak and movements disjointed. Your blood starts to become thicker and it's harder for your heart to pump it around the body, raising the heart rate and your blood pressure.

As time goes on the risk of delirium and unconsciousness increase. Eventually, you collapse and die. Of course, deprived of any water as I am, I'm peeing less, but eventually I'm forced to take a leak. The only place to do so is at the back of the shipping container, stepping into whatever filth is on the floor.

It's at times like this that I fall back on my training. I know the longer they keep me here, the less likely they are to release me without some significant gain. I now have to consider the 'what-ifs'. What if they offer me a drink, do I take it or might it be drugged? It's quite common in capture situations for captors to use some sort of narcotic to soften you up a little; to get you to talk; to admit to anything; to sign a bogus confession even. But if I don't drink I'm going to perish anyway. I figure I'll take a drink if I have to, in order to keep me alive. But not before then.

One of the lessons I learned in training is how to maintain

control over how the mind reacts to unusual and threatening situations. You have to be aware of how your body is at any given moment. If you accept a drink, but then start sensing that your eyes don't feel right, or you get other warning signs, such as dizziness, then your drink has very likely been spiked. You then know you've got to try to stay focused on keeping your mouth shut. It's important to tell yourself that your body and mind are reacting strangely because of a drug, while limiting your natural, emotional reactions. That way you can try to hold yourself together, even while you're under the influence of whatever it might be.

From outside, I hear the phone calls on my satphone start up again. By now, I don't doubt that each of these guys has made a call to their mother or their long-lost cousin in Outer Mongolia. They start dropping by every few minutes now, just to remind me how much trouble I'm in, and to take the opportunity to describe, with great relish, the conditions in their local prison. Not nice. They are clearly trying to scare me. I resign myself to sitting on the sticky, stinking floor, in a pool of sweat, and I start to feel drowsy. The heat's overwhelming and my mouth feels like the bottom of a parrot's cage. I'm wondering what's next, before I keel over from dehydration and heat exhaustion.

As the sun begins to drop towards the horizon, I somehow cling on to consciousness. I hear the door unlock and it creaks open. I've now been in this shithole for almost the entire day, and it shows. They lead me out and into the police station. I'm fully expecting my first proper beating, but this time I'm taken into another room, which looks a bit more high-powered and official. It's less of torture chamber, more a day-at-the-office kind of place.

They shove me down in a chair and this guy – who is pretty damn obese for an African – comes striding in. He makes his way to the desk and just about manages to squeeze in between the arms of his chair. Judging by the name plate on the desk, he's the chief of the police around here – so someone with some kind of decision-making power.

I'm pretty sure we've been through every possible question, so I can't imagine what he's going to ask of me now. Of course, I'm only too aware that in Togo, as in a lot of West Africa, white men of my age group, appearance and background are very much assumed to be mercenaries. Rightly or wrongly, we're often viewed as having brought harm to their countries. I guess it's only to be expected that they'll insist on sticking to that narrative, and dragging this whole affair out for as long as possible.

Desk Guy starts talking. In a low, rumbling kind of voice he tells me that I've entered Togo with illegal equipment and that this is a serious offence in their country. He stresses that mercenaries are dealt with harshly in Togo, and spends the next few minutes reading me the riot act. He finishes by saying that they're confiscating my passport and putting me under 'house arrest', at least until they can expel me from their country. Needless to say, the body armour and helmets will not be returned to me. I'm moving onto Stage Three of capture now, and this is far from being any kind of warm fluffy feeling.

With that I'm carted off, shoved in the back of another van and driven off to who-knows-where. At this stage, I don't have any real sense of what is going on or where I'm going. If Desk Guy was telling me the truth, they're convinced I'm a gun-for-hire and that

I am up to no good in their country, but they are still willing to let me leave Togo. That does not add up. Either way, we're moving onto Level Three of the capture process – where I'm going to be taken to somewhere seriously nasty, so they can lock me up for as long as they see fit.

When the van door opens, it's pretty near dark. I'm taken out and escorted into this pokey little hotel and shoved into one of the bedrooms. There's a policeman posted outside the door and several police cars parked up outside. I'm told they'll remain exactly where they are, to ensure I have no way of escaping. I will not be allowed to leave the hotel under any circumstances. They still have my passport, so I don't have much of a choice but to stay put.

I try to look for the upsides. At least I'm no longer locked up in that stinking shipping container, about to fry to death. I stumble to the bathroom and neck several gallons of water. I note that although the room isn't quite up to the standards of the Savoy, it is a little less sticky underfoot and does at least have a bed pushed against one wall. Having nothing better to do, I flake out and sleep the sleep of the utterly exhausted.

Come the morning, I'm wondering what on earth happens next – if and when I'll be allowed to return home – or, if this is some kind of deniable, secret detention centre, from where they might decide to quietly 'disappear' me. It strikes me that either is possible. Apart from mealtimes, I'm ordered to stay in my room. All I want to do is get out of Togo, either on a ship or a plane – I don't much care which – but I'm not allowed to move anywhere. It's the waiting around in limbo that's so soul-destroying.

I'm a prisoner in this room. At any moment someone in power

might change their mind. They could come here and drag me off down to the local prison and throw away the key. Or they could march me to the local execution block – their version of Chop-Chop Square. I try to engage in conversation with the guards. I ask them what's happening? When am I going to be allowed to return home? I get only surly, curt responses, which leave me none the wiser.

I'm wondering what's happened with Zero-Risk Security. Surely they must have cut some kind of deal by now? They return my satellite phone to me, but they may as well not have bothered. For some reason, I'm unable to get any kind of a connection. That night, I start to seriously consider my options. The longer you're held, the more it is a sign that your captors will hold onto you until they get exactly what they want. Trouble is, I just don't know what they're after. Are they trying to extract some serious ransom money? Or are they cutting a deal with one of the Islamist factions that terrorise West Africa? As I check through the window, there are still the two police cars parked up by the hotel entranceway. Outside my door sit the guards. For now at least, it looks as if I'm properly pinned down and hemmed in.

By the next morning there's still no sign of my release. I badger the guards. After a while, one of them seems to take pity on me. He reveals that the team at Zero-Risk have indeed been communicating with them. Apparently, they have managed to calm the situation down somewhat, by persuading the Togolese authorities that I'm not a mercenary intent on toppling their government. But if that's the case, then why am I still being detained?

I finally manage to get the satphone to work. I place a call to the

Zero-Risk office, but the two girls I speak to don't seem to have the slightest clue about what's happening. Why, if they want me out of the country, are the Togo authorities dragging their feet about my release, I ask? They don't seem to have any answers.

The next morning it's more of the same. The guards explain that I'm being held indefinitely, and nothing and no one seems to be doing anything to get me out of here. I call Zero-Risk's offices again, but again I'm left none the wiser. It feels as if I'm just being left to stew in my own sweat. Then, mid-morning, there's a knock on my door. Out of the blue several police have arrived. They announce they are there to take me to the airport.

As they escort me down to the police van and push me into the back, I'm still not sure if I'm going to make it. Maybe this is going to be a one-way ride to Chop-Chop Square. I figure the journey time should be the same as it was when I was taken from the airport to the shipping container. If it's any longer, I'll know they're taking me to another destination, at which stage I'll need to be ready to make a run for it.

If I do manage to escape, I'll then be faced with evading capture. Togo's not a large country, so with luck I could make it to the border. But the three neighbouring countries are not exactly the friendliest, and they're particularly unlikely to look kindly upon a wanted 'mercenary' running from one of their neighbours. As the drive begins I count out the time in my head, and I figure we've been on the road for just a little longer than the drive to the airport, when the van shudders to a halt. I'm tense and ready for anything as the doors swing open.

I get out, only to realise we are on the military side of the airport. I sense trouble, but there's a tight police escort marching to either side of me, and I'm propelled towards one of the main hangars. I'm only too aware how easy it would be for them to OBE me here, as we're well out of sight of the main airport and it's pretty deserted. It turns out that the military hangar has a back entrance leading into the civilian side of the airport. I'm taken from there to departures, whereupon I finally start to feel just a little less exposed and vulnerable. All I want right now is to get on a plane – any plane – and catch a flight to anywhere that isn't here.

I don't have any luggage to check in, as they've confiscated the body armour and helmets, leaving me just the one small holdall. I finally get my passport back. After a 90-minute wait in the airport lounge, still under heavy police guard, I'm escorted to a waiting plane – an Ethiopian Airlines flight, bound for London. While the police hang around to see that I don't scarper, I'm more concerned about checking who else may be aboard that flight and whether I may still be at risk. I make my observations of the other passengers, just try to ascertain if there are any plain-clothes Togolese intel types aboard. I can't see anyone who stands out, but who knows.

After forty minutes, the police officers make for the exit and shortly after the aircraft takes off. I have never been so glad to see the back of any country in my life. Togo is definitely off my holiday destination list. I've probably got a lifetime ban from the country, but I certainly don't intend to go back to ask. The body armour and the helmets are long gone, as is my anti-piracy contract – but at least I've got my freedom, and all my teeth and my other body parts are intact.

After a mission such as this one, that's about as good as it gets.

CHAPTER EIGHT

THE SUDAN

It was early 2008 when I got offered the chance to return to Africa on private security work, this time to the Sudan. By chance I'd bumped into a former SAS mate of mine who ran a private military company (PMC). He'd been asked to provide security for a French oil company who were having a spot of bother in one of Africa's most notorious war spots.

While they had concerns about their people based in Sudan's capital, Khartoum, they were having the greatest trouble on one of their rigs, set in the deep south of the country. It came complete with a good dose of argy-bargy from the local tribes, plus they had to deal with the regional police commander, who was apparently two sandwiches short of a picnic.

My mate asked me if I fancied flying out to Sudan, to see if I could help sort out all their problems. After my experiences in Togo, I sought a certain reassurance: I'd not be taking any military kit through Khartoum airport, by any chance? He confirmed that I'd be going in sanitised, and under the guise of being a health-and-safety officer. That being so, I told him I was happy to give it my best shot.

A couple of days later I lined up to board a flight to Khartoum, after which I'd take another into the south of the country, where the rig was moored on the White Nile, the lower part of the longest river in the world, the mighty Nile.

It was no exaggeration to say that Sudan was a nation in tatters. It had seen decades of civil war between the Arab-led Khartoum government in the largely-Muslim north, and the rebel forces of the mainly Christian and animist south. There had been numerous on-off peace agreements over the years, but basically the conflict had rumbled on from 1983 to 2005 – making it one of Africa's, and the world's, longest. It had resulted in the deaths of two million people from conflict, famine and disease – one of the highest death tolls of any war since the Second World War.

Typically, human rights violations were rife, including slavery, torture and mass killings. Entire generations had grown up knowing nothing but conflict and neglect, and the tension between Sudan's northern government and the southern rebels was at an all-time high. In short, this was a war-torn nation almost without compare, where they played by Big Boys' rules.

I'm heading out there just as tensions between the various factions are simmering away nicely and threatening to explode. The brief is that I'll be working as a 'solo operator' – carrying out a risk assessment on the company assets – mainly human – including devising strategies for extracting their personnel should things turn ugly . . . which I figure is only a matter of time.

Already, the troubles with the restive local tribespeople and the crazed local police commander are developing into a crisis all of their own. The tribe living in the vicinity of the rig are in the habit of pilfering anything they can get their hands on, while the police commander arrests anyone he can get his hands on, seemingly on a whim. The foreman of the site – known as the 'tool pusher' – has become the fall guy and is regularly getting flung into a great big festering pit dug into the ground, until the police commander's demands – no matter how bizarre or unreasonable – are met.

The oil company has decided enough is enough and want someone to sort it all out, keeping both the company property and its staff safe and secure. Now, as soon as you mention 'security' in countries like Sudan, where civil wars have been raging for years, officials tend to get edgy and have a tendency to refuse to let you in – hence my going in under the guise of being a 'health and safety officer'. I would have to act the part, whereas in reality I'd be focused entirely on security, security, security, and specifically, how to get the rig team out of there if it all turned very nasty.

Sudan was then the largest country in Africa, and the distances we were talking of having to cross if things went ugly were simply vast. Getting out of there was going to prove only half the problem. The local issues were just that: small scale and localised. But there had also been an upsurge in the fighting between the rebels and the Sudanese government forces further north, and trouble was beginning to kick off big time. The worries were that the rebels would try to take Khartoum. If they did, we'd have our only reliable route of escape via the airport closed off. Clearly, putting together an escape plan that would enable me and the staff to get out in one piece had to be my first priority.

The French company running the oil rig had their regional headquarters in Khartoum, so I headed there first, aiming to take a look at the security of one of their chief residences – a villa – set on the outskirts of the city.

Khartoum turned out to be a proper hell-hole. There was a seething groundswell of disquiet in the city and everyone was twitchy about what was going to happen. As a result it was a pretty unfriendly place, and even more so for any Westerner. With all the unrest, civic society seemed to be breaking down. The entire city appeared filthy, with trash everywhere, and people would regularly use the streets as a toilet. I was looking out the back of the villa shortly after my arrival and saw this guy walking by on the main road. He stopped, lifted up his dish-dash – Arab robe – and as bold as brass with people driving past in their cars, he crouched down and had a dump in full view of all.

Khartoum. It was that sort of city.

My arrival at the villa wasn't exactly a love-fest either. I was greeted by several of the oil company's management – all French nationals – who hadn't appeared at all happy to see me pitch up on their doorstep. The first night they took me to some restaurant in Khartoum, and hospitable though this was, there was no work being done, so we were just having a jolly really, or as much as you could bearing in mind the surroundings.

The next day I tried to get down to brass tacks – discussing their security issues, which were legion, and suggesting some strategies in the event of the city descending into madness and mayhem.

Unfortunately, they were having none of it: 'Non, non, non, it is all fine.'

It was clear they saw me as some unfortunate embuggerance. I tried convincing them otherwise. 'Guys, guys – listen. It is going to go seriously wrong in this country and you're going to thank me for my advice, mark my words.'

But there is just no telling some people. They think they are as safe as houses and just can't seem to comprehend the fact that the present unrest might explode and engulf the entire city, or how violent and ugly things can turn in an instant, especially in the middle of a civil war.

Despite this, I furnished them with all the instructions and strategies I believed they needed to get out in one piece. I couldn't be too heavy handed, especially as I was officially there as a 'health and safety officer', rather than the security expert that I am. But after a couple of days it was evident that I'd done all I could. It was time to head for the south of the country, to the actual rig itself, where the real and present danger was said to be most acute.

At that time Sudan was about *eight times* the size of the UK. Now, as a result of the civil war, it's split into two separate countries. The massive landmass consisted of a mix of arid desert, vast swamps and tropical rainforest. From Khartoum to the rig site was a good 500 miles or more, most of which was war-ravaged bush. Unsurprisingly, my journey to the rig proper would turn out to be a seriously convoluted and tortured affair.

In a dusty corner of Khartoum airport is an area where the charter flights operate. There, I found a rickety old aircraft that looked as if it should have been on display in the Khartoum Museum of Aviation (not that there is one). It bore a passing resemblance to a four-seater Cessna light aircraft, but it was a little bigger and a whole lot older and more decrepit than any Cessna I had ever seen. In fact, it was so ancient that I hadn't a clue what model it might be. Sure enough, it was to be the means via which I would make my onwards journey into the south of the country.

I'm not exactly a small bloke, and when I got inside the Khartoum Museum of Aviation showpiece, it started creaking and groaning as a rusting old caravan might. Saying a few muttered prayers mixed with curses, I sat down and went to belt up, but sure enough there weren't even any seat belts.

When flying into Pakistan, for onwards trips into Afghanistan, I'd often had to travel on Pakistan International Airlines (PIA). I'd been doing some private security work there, and me and my fellow operators had nicknamed PIA 'Prayers in the Air', for obvious reasons. But if there was ever an airline that deserved that moniker, the Khartoum Museum of Aviation airline is it.

I say a final prayer and we take to the skies – what else am I to do?

It proves one hell of a bumpy, windy, engine-coughing, heart-stopping ride, but eventually we make it, touching down on this single dirt-strip that is your typical 'airport' in the midst of the Sudanese bush. I ask the obvious question: *Are we there yet?* Not a chance. This is just the start of things . . . From here I have to catch my next flight, which will take me to the actual rig itself, at its mooring on the White Nile. The only airframes in view that might possibly be airworthy seem to be four Soviet-era Mil Mi8 Hip transport helicopters, which are painted in the distinctive white livery of the United Nations.

One of the – somewhat mystifying – briefs I've been given before undertaking this trip is to bring a utility strap – a belt of super-tough material, with a secure buckle – with me for 'the flights'. I soon find out why. Sure enough, one of the Hips is to be my next mode of transport, but when I clamber into the back of the beast I discover all of the floorboards are missing. Where there should be a floor is just one big open hole. Flying with no floor lends a whole different dimension to the Prayers in the Air experience. Still, at least I'll get a good look at the scenery.

While there are four of these Hips present, only one is even vaguely serviceable – the one with the missing floor. The others are being cannibalised for their spare parts, in an effort to keep this one in the air. And the utility strap – no guessing what that is for anymore. It's so I can lash myself to the side of the helo's hold, to prevent myself from falling . . .

I sit myself down and just when I'm thinking it can't get any worse, I meet the pilot, Viktor, who's Russian. He reeks of vodka, and he is clearly as pissed as a newt, and so it transpires is his co-pilot, Boris. If I think about this for much longer, the truth is I'll disembark the helo and jump at a flight back north, courtesy of Khartoum Museum of Aviation airlines.

Instead, I fashion my utility strap into the nearest approximation of a seat belt I can manage, given my mode of transport has no floor, and I clip myself onto the side of the Hip. As you can imagine, I've flown in a lot of helicopters in my time, both military and civilian. At one time, in Iraq, I was in a Puma when a surface-to-air missile went flaming past the open side door, spitting-distance close to the fuselage. Someone happened to be filming at the time, and the flame-yellow exhaust of the missile is clearly visible on the video, as is the look of shock and consternation of those riding in the helo's hold.

But, take it from me, for sheer crazed death-wish insanity, our flight across the swamps of Sudan in that floorless Hip piloted by a pair of pissed Russians knocks that Iraqi Lynx ride into a cocked hat.

Eventually, we decelerate in a hideous clanking of decrepit turbines and aging rotor-blades, as the Hip flares out over a vast expanse of what looks like mangrove swamp. At first, I can't see where on earth Viktor and Boris think there's firm enough ground to make a landing. But as we lose altitude and the swamp rushes up to meet us, I spy a tiny raised platform of flattened terrain, which looks like a small man-made island.

The Hip touches down, and with the rotors still turning and burning I unclip and dash off, heading across a narrow walkway that looks as if it leads to the accommodation buildings. As I leave, Viktor and Boris give me a vodka-fuelled waive from the cockpit, and flash the V for victory signs, before the Hip claws and clanks its way skywards once more. Upon reflection, I guess if I had to fly that thing daily across Sudan, I'd probably end up hitting the bottle myself. So no hard feelings.

It turns out the rig itself is made up of two sites: the drilling area and the accommodation block. Basically, the latter consists of nothing more than a load of shipping containers not much bigger than my erstwhile Togo prison cell, bolted together and placed aboard a massive rusting barge. Four storeys high and about the same deep, it looks like a giant floating container ship that has somehow made it this far up the White Nile. With that moored off one area of the riverbank, the rig proper lies around a vast, sweeping bend , and you could travel between the two on the company launch.

There is no way on or off the accommodation barge other than by boat, meaning you have to travel everywhere by water. If things do turn noisy with the rebels, I am going to need an exit plan for the company staff and myself which takes into account the logistical challenges of living on a container ship moored on the White Nile, several hundred miles from anywhere that could vaguely be considered as 'civilisation'. Some challenge.

I meet some of the crew and get introduced to my 'roommate', an arrangement that I am not exactly enamoured with. After just completing the journey from hell, I'd hoped at least to have my own shipping container to myself. Instead, I have to share it with a French guy who is apparently a medical doctor, but who looks as if one month too many out here has totally fried his brain. The only way to communicate seems to be by using hand signals, with some added facial expressions.

Later that evening I decide on what my strategy is going to be. Desperate times call for desperate measures. I'm going to eat as much junk food as I possibly can and fart as much as is humanly possible, so my 'roommate' gets half gassed to death in the shipping container. Sure enough that is exactly what I do. I fill the interior with an odour that strikes me as being a blend of rotting eggs and fermented cabbage. The next morning my 'roommate' moves out and from then on he sleeps at his surgery. I get the shipping container to myself, which is about as good as it gets out here.

I catch the launch for a ride to the rig. There, I meet the guy in charge – the 'tool pusher' or foreman – who turns out to be an Indian called Rajesh Bhargave. Rajesh is the one who's been getting all the agro off the local police commander, who's in the habit of throwing him into a hole in the ground and holding him there until he gets whatever he wants. Bearing in mind that I've come onto this job supposedly as a health and safety officer, Rajesh gets me straight onto a few health and safety issues right away. But I can see he knows that I haven't got a clue what I'm doing. It's not long before he pulls me into his office for a quiet word. He asks me outright – what am I really doing here? I give him some cock-and-bull story to try to maintain my cover, but I can tell it doesn't wash.

Rajesh looks me dead in the eye. 'Look, mate, I've never seen a worse health and safety operator in my life. You don't know the first thing about health and safety, no offence intended.'

At this point I'm still weighing him up, and trying to assess if I should level with him. Bearing in mind everything that's happened to date on this trip, I figure Rajesh is semi-okay. I venture to give him at least some of the truth. I tell him I'm here to make an assessment, part health and safety, but big part security too. I stress that the word 'security' doesn't go down too well in a place like this, where they all immediately think you're a Rambo-esque gun for hire – a dreaded 'mercenary'.

Fortunately, Rajesh gets it. He seems perfectly okay with what I'm trying to do here. Very likely he's thinking that with me on station, there's maybe a little less chance of the police commander throwing him in the pit anytime soon.

Rajesh offers to shows me round the rig. As he does so, he explains the trouble they've been having with the village tribespeople, most of whom are armed. They have a habit of boarding the rig and nicking everything and anything they can lay their hands on: clothing, boots and all kinds of drilling gear. They are one of his chief headaches. The other is the lunatic police commander. He's making regular demands of the staff – insisting they hand over items of personal or monetary value, such as tools, batteries, pairs of boots or cash. When he doesn't get what he wants, he grabs Rajesh and throws him in the pit. It's basically your typical ten-foot deep hole dug in the ground, with a grill over the top. And there Rajesh stays, until all the demands are met.

It's sheer extortion and bribery.

Because of the ever-present threat of becoming a guest in the pit, Rajesh has taken to locking himself in his office, just in case, which makes it very difficult for him to do his job. The oil company has decided that enough is enough, and they want someone to stand up to the police chief's outrageous behaviour. They also want to find a way to keep the locals in check, keeping them well away from the rig and their staff. Having let slip that I am not really a health and safety officer, Rajesh thinks that on both counts I am the man for the job.

When I finally get to meet the police chief, he introduces himself with a name which sounds to me like 'Commander Maggot', although I'm the first to admit that I am not that familiar with surnames in the depths of the Sudan. I'm kind of thinking *that fits* – that's what I'll nickname him – before he explains that in his tribe, the word 'maggot' (and I'm spelling it phonetically here, obviously) actually means a 'very long-horned bull' . . . And of course, long-horned cattle are revered in this part of the world as a symbol of status and wealth.

Mr. Maggot looks to be in his forties and has the distinctive scars on his forehead – parallel lines arranged in a shallow V – which mark him out as being from the Dinka tribe, one of the most numerous in Southern Sudan. He's dressed head to toe in a red Nike tracksuit, and it's on the tip of my tongue to ask him where his uniform is? But by past form, that might be enough to land me a spell in the pit, which I am anxious to avoid.

Mr. M explains that while he has an 'official role' in the local police force, it doesn't seem to come with very much kit. I figure he's like a British special constable, so a volunteer bobby, but minus the clothes, helmet, truncheon and radio that tend to come with it. No doubt, Mr. M is pushing at the limits of his authority, but who around here is ever going to challenge him or call him out? In short, he's master and commander of his own small domain in the absolute middle of bloody nowhere.

With great pride, he escorts me down to the shack which serves as his base of operations, revealing 'the pit', which is his equivalent of a jail cell. It even has a live victim inside it right now. As I gaze down, I see he's got one of the locals held prisoner in there. Mr M points and gestures and laughs conspiratorially, as if having that guy incarcerated in the pit is the most natural thing in the world and the next best thing to the Christmas panto around here. I'm not quite sure if this is a show for my benefit, or whether Mr. M is genuinely this warped – but either way, I'm not impressed. Despite his hail-fellow-well-met act, I can tell Mr. M is on the war path.

I sense trouble lurking big time just around the bend of the White Nile.

CHAPTER NINE

EXIT STRATEGY

I figure Mr. M is primed to blow at the slightest excuse. The guy is as mad as a box of frogs, and twice as dangerous. If the launch that transports the workers to and from the rig happens to so much as to put a ripple in the water which unsettles his canoe, he comes storming onto the rig to seize someone.

Unsurprisingly, everybody seems on the make around here. With Mr. M it's hardly very smart or subtle. It's a case of: *if you want me to release your man, what are you going to give me in return?* Rajesh explains how Mr. M once demanded 20 pairs of boots. Rajesh explained that he didn't have 20 pairs of boots to spare, so Mr. M dragged him off and stuck him in the pit. There Rajesh stayed, until his colleagues had no choice but to pay Mr. M off with 20 pairs of boots, which meant any number of them had no work footwear.

Poor Rajesh has any number of similar stories. If it wasn't Mr. M trying a bit of pit-related extortion and bribery, it was the local tribes lifting whatever they could off the rig. It was a natural magnet for them, because of all the modern kit, technology and activity it housed. Often, they would just appear out of thin air and take anything they could find.

I could see the evidence of such light-fingered work all around. I'd spot a group of locals wondering around, wearing rig-workers' safety goggles. Some were made of clear plastic, but the real sought-after numbers had a noticeable tint to them. The locals seemed to think they were genuine sunglasses, so I'd see these guys stalking about like they were some kind of chilled-out US gangster rapper – like 2Pac – wearing tinted safety goggles.

The oil company has cut a deal with the local community that a certain number have to be employed on rig-related work. Rajesh explains that managing that is in itself a nigh-on fulltime job. One day, he sacked one of the locals because he kept going off to have a nap in the shade of a big pile of pipes. Within hours, twenty of his tribe had turned up in their dug-out canoes, threatening to wreak havoc and chaos as a result of the sacking. They wanted their man reinstated and weren't in any mood to argue. So Rajesh gave him a made-up job. He became the 'brush man', and his responsibility was to properly maintain all the bristles of the brooms on the rigs.

It was ridiculous. In a way it was pathetic – for it reflected how desperate the locals were for any kind of gainful employment. But most of all, it made a mockery of any kind of security on the rig. I'd been sent here to sort out such issues, and I figured this was first and foremost a hearts-and-minds kind of challenge. Accordingly, I came up with a suitable plan, one predicated on a good dollop of lateral-thinking and a huge slice of can-do attitude.

I started fishing off the rig. In part it gave me something relaxing to do, in between dealing with the war-like local tribespeople and the lunatic police chief. I have always loved to fish. I first caught the bug while running wild from the kids' homes, and living off the land in the New Forest. Then, catching a trout meant a good and nutritious – and free – meal. Since that time I've fished for 'snow trout' and a fish called the common miranka, in the Bamian River, in Afghanistan; and I've fished for tuna, barracuda and sailfish in the Red Sea, in between stints protecting merchant ships from Somali pirates. I've even considered putting in an application with Guinness World Records for fishing the world's most dangerous stretches of water.

Being a bit of a fishing nut, I always take some line and hooks with me on any such job. The White Nile proves a fisherman's paradise. The plentiful supply of Nile perch, catfish and tigerfish means I'm able to pull 'em out one after another and fill a basket in no time. I decide that whenever some of the locals appear, aiming to pilfer some ridiculous piece of kit off the rig, I'll offer them some fish instead. It sounds insane, but in hearts-and-minds work sometimes you just have to meet one kind of insanity with another.

It doesn't take me long to catch my daily quota of fish, and I love doing it. In no time I've got the locals turning up for their midday fish ration, after which they tend to leave us and the rig well alone. My bizarre hearts-and-minds programme – one based around the cold-blooded, slimy, scaly beasts of the Nile – proves a real hit.

But there is a saying, isn't there: *Give a man a fish and you feed him for a day. Teach a man to fish and you feed him for a lifetime.* I can't remember when I first heard it, but I'm a big fan of such sentiment. In fact, my life embodies that message. The British military didn't just give me a fish, they taught me all the how-to. I learned the skills of elite soldiering, which enabled me to build a life and a career off the back of it.

More to the point, I've got some sympathy for the locals. I really have. Had I been born into the Dinka tribe and brought up in such a god-forsaken, war-torn patch of bush in the absolute middle of nowhere, with zero prospects of ever getting out or of anything much ever changing, I'd very likely be pilfering whatever I could off the white man's oil rig, even if I didn't really understand what any of it was for.

So, I start teaching them how to fish. To me, it beggars belief that they could have lived on the banks of the Nile since time immemorial and not have learned to fish, but there it is. To be fair, they are quick and enthusiastic learners and I soon have them plucking big Nile species out of the water, and loving every minute of it. It is great for gaining trust. And believe it or not it even works with Mr. M . . .

Admittedly, he proves a little more challenging to talk around, but eventually I crack even him. Whenever he comes onto the rig, ranting and raving about so-and-so needing a spell in the pit, I suggest we go sit by the water and chat about just what his problem is. As if absentmindedly, I'd bait a line and throw it in, before asking him: 'So, what can we do to end this situation?' I take great care never to say: What can we give you to make you happy. It should always be: *What can we do to end this situation?*

Thing is, when you're fishing and the line goes taut and you've got a massive mystery beast on the far end, all talk of the pit and bribes goes out of the window, as all hands get busy hauling the thing in. Nile perch can grow up to two metres in length and weight over 200 kg, and in the White Nile there are some big old monsters. Even a total madman like Mr. M isn't immune to the thrills of hauling one of those beasts in.

In time, I persuade him to join me in singing the Bob the Builder children's song, 'Big Fish, Little Fish, Cardboard Box', complete with all the hand gestures and the silly dance that goes with it. I convince Mr. M that it is a revered British ritual performed before fishing in order to bless the catch. Truth be told, I roar with laughter inside, every time I succeeded in making him sing the 'Big Fish' song with me. But I figure as he is so keen on slamming people into his pit, it's the least he deserves.

My fishing-based hearts-and-minds programme takes up a fair chunk of my time, but I don't mind. It's great being out in the open. Even the journey by launch each morning, from the accommodation to the rig, is a chance to see kingfishers dipping low across the water and darting in and out of the reeds, plus these big old crocodiles lurking on the sandbanks, waiting for their morning feed.

But one day I'm perched on the edge of the rig, line in the drink, when I am assailed by the most awful stink I've ever smelled in my life. It is as if something has died and all that is left is a rotting putrid carcass, and I'm getting the rancid smell of its decomposing flesh pressure-washed into my nostrils. It is infinitely worse than the Togo shipping container, and that's saying something.

I see a local approaching in his little canoe. As he nears me the stench gets stronger and stronger. I can see the crocodiles in the bush on either side of the river with their eyes lighting up, as their noses dip into the water excitedly and they launch themselves in his direction. Clearly, to a croc this is the most appetising smell in the world. But I'm starting to feel real queasy, wondering if my breakfast is going to make a reappearance.

The local reaches the edge of the rig, and the crocodiles have formed a semi-circle in the water to his rear. When I peer over the side to take a look, I see what looks like a great big leg lying in the bottom of his canoe. It's the largest I have ever laid my eyes on, complete with massive toe-nails poking out the end. At the other extremity lies what looks like the thigh of whatever creature he's butchered, and the thing can barely fit in his boat.

All of a sudden I realise what it is. He has the entire leg of an adult hippo lying in his boat. 'What – on earth – is that?' I shout, pulling a face and trying not to wretch. 'You're not suggesting anyone *eats* it, are you?'

'No, no,' he yells back. 'Is good meat. Very tasty.'

'Good meat? You're havin' a laugh. That is . . . honking.'

'No, no. Freshly killed this morning.'

'Freshly killed? That leg hasn't seen its owner for the best part of several weeks!'

He does his best to sell me the equivalent of several hundred hippo burgers, but I am absolutely not buying. Eventually, I convince him to sling his hook and I watch him paddle off downriver, with a phalanx of crocodiles in hot pursuit, their snouts poised ready to snap. Whether his hippo leg landed him in serious trouble or not I don't know, but I never saw the guy again, that's for sure.

With the first phase of Operation Hippo Leg somehow pulled off, I figure I need a few days break in the UK, to de-stress and de-compress. A week later I fly back into Khartoum, to launch Operation Hippo Leg II. Things are really hotting up down at the rig, and I have to get back there pronto. Once more I board the Khartoum Museum of Aviation airlines wreck, and prepare for the bone-shaking journey from hell. But today, the aircraft has a different flight crew.

Today, I'm blessed with Dimitri and his co-pilot, Igor and, sur-prise, surprise – they're both drunk as skunks. As we set off down the runway, the plane begins to shake and rattle as never before. We're jumping and jolting down the strip like a bucking bronco on acid. Somehow, Dimitri and Igor manage to coax the aircraft into the air, but they can't seem to gain any proper height. I notice we are rapidly approaching a series of low-rise buildings, and we're flying along at about their rooftop level. In fact we're so low that I'm able to follow the route they're taking via the roads. It's like map-reading, only we're in a plane some thirty feet above the ground.

We approach the city and I'm thinking, *we aren't getting any higher.* I can identify some of the key landmarks, including the Farouq Cemetery, which we're likely to end up in at this rate. Dimitri and Igor begin to weave and swerve their way through the buildings to either side. One wrong move by those drunken lunatics and it's going to be curtains for all of us. My brain is des-perately trying to grapple with what on earth they can be playing at. Have they had so much to drink that they're totally incapable of flying this thing? Or are they so totally smashed they're planning to shunt us into the side of a building, suicide style? Do I need to try to wrestle control of the plane off them and fly it myself?

All of a sudden, there is a dramatic surge upwards and Dimitri and Igor manage to clear the tallest of the buildings in our path, but only just. They've managed to gain enough height to do a slow, laborious loop back to Khartoum airport, where they bring us back down to land.

After prising myself out of my seat, I go and ask Dimitri what the hell just happened? Despite his thick Russian-accent and his thicker vodka-slur, I gather that he's claiming there is bad weather at our destination, so he's been forced to turn back. I give him the look that says I know he is talking a crock of shite. He changes tack, arguing he wasn't able to fly any higher, in case we got hit by a commercial airliner. *Yeah, right, Dimitri.*

I finally manage to get to the rig by ditching Dimitri and Igor and landing myself a half-sober aircrew instead. Right away, I detect a definite shift in the atmosphere. There's a whole lot more menace in the air. It's time to put an exit plan into place and to make ready our getaway. That, I decide, has to be the entire focus and thrust of Operation Hippo Leg II.

During the time I've been away, tensions have reached boiling point between the Sudanese government forces and the opposition rebels, the JEM (Justice and Equality Movement), situated in the west of the country, in a region called Darfur. There have been a series of murderous and deadly air and ground attacks, as the government forces have hunted down the JEM rebels, killing, raping and enslaving civilians across a vast swathe of territory. It's caused a mass exodus of civilians from Darfur – displacing millions, most of whom are families with children.

The resulting tension and anger have swept the country like wildfire, inflaming all of the rebel forces against the regime in Khartoum. Within days of my return, serious fighting starts to break out, but this time it's spreading towards the very centre of the country, and threatening to engulf the capital. I call the French team based in the head office, in Khartoum, and tell them what should be blindingly obvious: those security and evacuation procedures I outlined last time I was there – it's time to start putting them in to action.

Around the rig I've noticed a significant build-up of troops – policemen actually wearing uniforms, plus soldiers. They start paying us visits aboard the rig. Ironically, whenever Mr. M's police colleagues turn up, our local 'tracksuit plod' does a vanishing act. The increase in all this military and paramilitary activity is a sure-fire combat indicator; a signifier that it's all poised to blow. My sole focus now has to be preparing a path off the rig and to safety for the oil company's crew.

I put in place a communications schedule with the office, in Khartoum, so that at a certain time each day I will attempt to raise them via my satellite phone. I doubt if they'll reveal to me the full extent of how bad things are getting up north, as we've never exactly hit it off, but they are one of my few sources of intel. Other than that, I'm left to rely on radio news bulletins via the BBC World Service, or any information I can gain off the locals – mostly, those I've befriended via my hearts-and-minds fishing programme.

I can't be too obvious with my questioning. Asking people if they've seen any extra government troops, or any signs of rebels fighters massing in the area, is sure to raise suspicions. Instead, I aim to drop a few questions into the conversation subtly, hoping I can squeeze some info out of them while landing the odd Nile perch or two.

Rajesh is regularly speaking with HQ, so I monitor his phone calls for any significant developments. Fortunately, I have unlimited access to all areas of the rig, so I can sit on the platform at the back of his office, apparently sunning myself, but in reality ear-wigging his phone-calls. I have to be really careful. This sort of stuff basically amounts to spying on people, and in these kinds of countries being accused of 'spying' can get you locked up and the key very much thrown away. But I am desperate for intelligence and I need to use whatever means I can.

If the rebel forces are to take Khartoum, that poses a massive problem for all of us. Even if we can get off the rig and reach that dusty airstrip where the UN have their lone helo, we can go no further if Khartoum airport is under siege or blocked. That means our key exit route out of the country will be closed to us. And what will happen if we can't even get to the UN helipad, which is a very real possibility?

For sure, we needed an alternative safe route out for the crew and for me. The fall-back plan I developed is this: we'll use the two motor launches that served the rig as a means of escape, and to avoid any armed conflict that is spreading across the north. That will mean motoring south down the White Nile, even though that presents its own risks, as we will be moving further into rebel-held territory. But I figure it has to be a viable alternative.

Still under my guise of 'health and safety', I get the launch drivers to give me lessons in how their craft operate. That done, I start to build up fuel and water caches, hidden on the banks of the river, but which can be easily accessed. I collect together satellite imagery and maps of the country, which will enable me to chart the fastest and most direct route out. But even with the best preparations in the world, a journey by the river is unlikely to be plain sailing. Everywhere the local tribes are present, and they all have boats of one kind or another. How will they react to a mystery party steaming into their domain, unannounced? How will the rebels react to our surprise arrival?

The end-point of any journey has to be Kenya, a relatively stable country lying to the south of Sudan. If push comes to shove and Khartoum airport closes, we'll have no other choice but to travel by river. So I need to refine that plan of escape. I figure I can entice the launch drivers on to the rig, using some porn as the eye-candy to get them there, and some beers to keep them compliant. I'll get them nice and tipsy and bedded in, before locking them into my shipping container and stealing away with one of their launches, which I'll load up with supplies from my hidden caches.

Then I'll head off down the Nile with myself at the wheel, and with the members of the company crew aboard. Escape and evasion were a key part of my military training, and long before that it was something I'd perfected during my time in the kids' homes. Back then I was always looking for ways to get away; anything to avoid feeling trapped; anything to ensure my freedom. I'd learned to survive in the wild, creating my own shelters, finding food and warmth, and basically living off my wits. All my life I've been weighing up my environments, and looking for escape routes and how to survive. It means I consider every possibility, and prepare, prepare, prepare.

But as I'm still operating under the guise of health and safety, I have to be careful. I have to be circumspect with what I tell Rajesh and the other company crew, but I'm keen to put preparations in place. I decide I'll tell the crew as little as possible, but that doesn't mean that I won't start directing them. Most likely, they will never have faced an evacuation before. I need them to be in a state of readiness, so when the time comes we can bale out quickly and calmly. But I'm also mindful that with the local tribes and police being so near at hand, if they get wind of my intentions they will cause no end of trouble, which could scupper any escape attempt.

One of my top priorities is to prepare a grab sack for everyone, if we have to evacuate. It needs to be ready, packed and hidden somewhere each of the crew can snatch it quickly, when the time comes. This will include a 24-hour survival kit – emergency food, navigation equipment and a few little bits and pieces to get someone out of trouble. It will contain water rations and items of non-perishable but nutritious foods. There'll be some means of fire-making and a waterproof cape, to stay dry. There will also be a torch, a compass and a map of the local area.

If we evacuate by boat down the White Nile, we will very likely have to proceed on foot at some stage. One challenge we'll face is that the further south we proceed, the more we'll get into serious jungle, so choosing our best route will be critical.

One of the key things I learned about in the military is choosing an emergency rendezvous (ERV). It might be a specific spot that everyone has to get to before reorganizing and then moving off again. In war-torn countries like Sudan, it's all too easy to get overrun by warring factions. That might mean we'll be forced to withdraw to some area away from our chosen route, to avoid such confrontations, before we can move on again. I need to have a good idea of the terrain we'll have to cross and the likely problems we might face, together with several alternative routes to safety. I'm convinced it will be only a matter of time before events escalate and we'll have to make a dash for safety.

Within a day or so the inevitable happens: troop numbers increase massively and we start to receive more and more visits from police and soldiers. In a call with the team at headquarters in Khartoum, they tell me that violence has broken out less than 200 miles away from the city, as rebels clash with government troops. There is increasing unrest on the outskirts of the capital, and it's time for them to get the hell out of there.

I figure we need to do the same down at the rig, and while we still can. Now is the time for everyone to leave. This is a spur-of-the-moment decision, which means there's no last-minute faffing around with crew grabbing clothing and personal effects and God-knows-what. I can't afford to have anything hinder our safe exit. I get the UN helicopter to fly into the man-made island, bundle the crew members into it and we lift off and get flown out of there.

Thankfully, by the time we reach Khartoum airport, it is still operating a handful of international flights. The crew take the first they can that's heading back to France, and I catch the only one remaining that's bound for the UK. We get out literally by the skin of our teeth.

Once back in London, I discover that even as we were flying out of Khartoum, the rebels were fast approaching, reaching to a point just ten miles to the west of the city. As the next 24 hours unfold, they mount an attack on Khartoum, temporarily seizing control, while targeting military bases and police stations. Heavy fighting rages on the streets around the Arabic market of Al-Souq Al-Arabi, only 2 miles from the airport. Government forces launch air strikes on the rebels, as they make a push towards the presidential palace. Civilians are shot on the streets amid tumultuous violence.

The capital, including the airport, comes under a dusk-to-dawn curfew, as the battles for control rages. Thankfully, the crew and I escaped in the nick of time. All the preparations had paid off. Despite the French team in the head office thinking I was paranoid with all my warnings, they had got out safe and sound as well. As a bonus, we'd avoided having to brave the boat journey south, which in truth I had not been relishing at all.

Operation Hippo Leg II had succeeded – in that all of us lived to see another day.

CHAPTER TEN

STRIKING GOLD

Shortly after my Sudan job I was contracted by British gold-mining company Bullion Resources Ltd, to advise on security for their operations. Again, as sod's law would have it, I was about to be dispatched to deepest darkest Africa.

Guinea is a country on the hot and steamy coast of tropical West Africa, and it has a fearsome history of lawless instability. In 2000, a series of border attacks from rebels in neighbouring Liberia and Sierra Leone threatened to plunge the country into civil war, causing violent instability that rumbled on for years. And then in 2008, Lansana Conte, Guinea's president of nearly twenty-five years, died, ushering in a military coup – kind of par for the course, for this part of Africa.

Captain Moussa Dadi Camara decided to seize power, arguing that Guinea's rampant poverty and corruption had to be ended, and that he was the man for the job ... By the following year demands for Camara to step down were sweeping the country and about to erupt into widespread violence. On the 28 September 2009, following demonstrations in the capital, Conakry's football stadium by his opponents, Camara dispatched the 'Red Berets' – his elite presidential guard – to deal with the 'uprising'.

The result was a vicious blood bath, with civilians shot, knifed and bayonetted indiscriminately by the Red Berets and women brutally gang-raped.

Hundreds were left dead and injured.

By the start of the following year – 2010 – the people of Guinea were desperate to topple Camara at all costs. The people at Bullion Resources were worried sick that more savagery and unrest was on the cards, unleashing a world of trouble their way. With the old adage that prevention is better than cure, they decided they wanted someone with an elite forces background and experience in war torn countries to sort their security – hence their approach to me.

For Bullion Resources it was less about trying to protect monetary assets at the mine, and more about saving human lives. If things turned seriously nasty, Guinea was the kind of place where you could easily get abducted and have your kidneys cut out and sold to the highest bidder.

Not without a little trepidation, I packed my bags in preparation for heading into Africa's dark heart . . . again. I flew out to Bamako-Senou International Airport in the centre of Mali, my stop-over for the onwards leg to Guinea. I'd been told to overnight there at a specific hotel, after which I'd meet Mick White, one of Bullion Resources' in-country managers, who would drive me down to the mine itself.

It was the first time I'd been to Bamako, Mali's capital city, and initial impressions were ones of pleasant surprise: there was a real French feel to the place. I checked into my hotel and discovered it had a very chic-looking al fresco dining area out front, complete with fancy, wrought-iron chairs. I made a beeline for it, almost feeling as if I'd stepped into some Parisienne café that had been transplanted to Africa.

All in all, it was actually very nice.

After a decent bite to eat I decided to check out the hotel bar. I don't know what it is about bars in West Africa, but they're always heaving. Sure enough, this one was jammed and noisy as hell, plus judging by the scantily-clad women lounging all over the place, full of ladies-of-the-night. I'd barely managed to get a first beer down me before this girl with ridiculously long legs and a skirt that left nothing to the imagination practically plonked herself on my lap.

'Sorry love, I'm already taken.'

'Ahhh, noooo,' she purred, looking hopeful that I'd change my mind.

'Yep, and the missus is the jealous type. The last woman that plonked her arse on my lap ended up in hospital.'

With that she slid off to the next bar stool, leaving me to have a few more beers in relative peace and quiet.

The next morning I treated myself to the hotel breakfast, tucking into an English-style fry-up of bacon, sausage and eggs. The bread, a French stick, was absolutely gorgeous – as good as any I'd ever had in France. I've always said that you can judge a country on how well it can make bread, because let's face it, if they can't make bread what chance have they got? So far this trip had been surprisingly enjoyable, but something told me it couldn't last . . .

With a hearty breakfast down me, I was ready for the off, and with perfect timing I got a call from Mick that he was downstairs in reception. He turned out to be an Aussie, and a good bit taller than me but about half my size in width. In fact, he looked a lot like the proverbial bean pole but he seemed amiable-enough. I followed him out to his 4x4, chucked my luggage in the boot and off we set.

Mick informed me that it was nearly a two-hour drive from Bamako to Siguiri, in the Kankan region, and the site of Bullion Resources' key mining assets in Guinea, so plenty of time to get the lowdown on the company and the job. He let slip that they'd previously contracted an ex-Marine to manage security, but he'd turned out to be worse than useless, so they'd edged him out, and I was now getting shoehorned in. At least that was Mick's side of the story: for all I knew the former Marine could have been shit-hot, and Bullion Resources had failed to heed any of his advice, opting to get shot of him instead of making some tough decisions. It wouldn't be the first time in my experience.

As I've already mentioned, most of Africa really doesn't warm to the word 'security', let alone anyone actively employed to provide specialist 'security services'. Unsurprisingly, Mick confirmed that I'd be working under the guise of a 'health and safety officer' – yet again – despite the fact that I know as much about health and safety as a tree surgeon knows about brain surgery. This time I also had the added bonus of the handy title of 'local liaison officer' – whatever that might signify.

Mick explained that Bullion Resources' main business was exploratory mining, which meant they were drilling boreholes to detect sizeable quantities of gold and diamonds. Once a deposit was found and the area secured, another company came in to carry out the extraction work. According to Mick, mining was huge in Guinea. Despite the evident poverty of its people, the country was rich in minerals and it was pulling in international investment from all over the world. Countries like China were desperate for raw materials to up their manufacturing capacity. The main problem was that foreign countries were seen as intent on exploiting Guinea's natural resources, while giving back little in terms of investment in social or economic infrastructure.

It had given mining a bad name.

As Mick spoke, I was starting to get a better sense of the root causes of Bullion Resources' problems. If any kind of civil unrest kicked off, the mines could well become a target for a whole lot of aggression, as pent-up frustrations and resentment boiled to the surface – hence them calling me in to come up with some strategies to safeguard their staff.

After driving for an hour on a fairly decent highway, we turned off the main drag and continued on a series of bumpy dirt tracks, until finally pulling onto the stretch of road that led into the mining area itself. It turned out to be a surprisingly decent patch of tarmac. Mick told me it had been paid for by the mining company, to ensure its employees could get in and out relatively quickly and without too many problems. But that hadn't stopped the locals attempting to make money out of it any which way they could.

Mick warned me that dotted along the road were makeshift 'checkpoints' manned by a bizarre combination of police, plus the local militia, which included scores of child soldiers. He stressed that if ever I needed to travel the road it was best to do so in the morning, because by the afternoon the adults were off their heads on drugs, leaving the kids in charge. He warned that it didn't take a lot to rile them and you could easily find yourself in real trouble – face down in the African dust, a boot in the small of your back and a gun muzzle jammed into the back of your skull.

Fortunately, it was still relatively early by the time Mick and I ran 'Checkpoint Alley'. As we flashed past a couple of the make-shift roadblocks I noticed – with a certain sinking feeling – that each had a steel shipping container positioned to one side. With less than pleasant memories of my Togo incarceration coming to mind, I asked Mick what they were for.

He laughed, a little insanely, it struck me: 'That's where they stick you if you cause trouble. Too much trouble too late in the afternoon, and they'll roast you alive in there . . .'

Apparently, the standard punishment in Guinea for getting pinged on a checkpoint was being locked up inside one of those containers for a good few hours under the blistering sun. It seemed as if the methods of the Togolese police were spreading far and fast. As I'd seen both there and in Sudan, it appeared to be standard practice in Africa to stick you in a baking-hot container or a stinking, sodden hole in the ground on even the slightest pretext. I wasn't entirely surprised that Guinea was no different.

It's impossible to grasp the size of these mines until you actually see one for yourself. When I first caught a glimpse of this one, I was gobsmacked at the sheer scale of the place. It was absolutely colossal. You could fit at least four Wembley Stadiums into just this one mine.

As I peered down into the abyss, trucks full of what looked like earth were crawling all over the site like ants. As we got closer, I was shocked at just how huge those vehicles were. Each wheel must have been almost the height of a London double-decker bus. It was like we'd fallen into a land of giants, with everything scaled up in size accordingly. As I watched the trucks rumble around the site, I didn't even want to think about the outcome if a bunch of irate locals broke into the mine and tried to hijack one of those brutes. Carnage is putting it mildly.

We reached the company compound on the outskirts of the gold mine blissfully unmolested. The employees were accommodated in rows of traditional-looking huts, which Bullion Resources had managed to make semi-liveable. They were basically your mud-walled one-room circular building, with a thatched conical roof topping it off, and a side area for the bathroom. Inside there was just about enough space to swing a cat, or to get your head down after a hard day's graft in the mine.

In an effort to keep the mine workers sweet, there was a decent cookhouse, Mick explained, plus a swimming pool, a 24/7 bar, and a massive fleet of vehicles. It was an impressive set-up, but I felt obliged to ask the obvious question: why the 24-hour, seven-days-a-week bar? Apparently, all the drillers at the mine were Aussies and they worked shifts – 12 hours on and 12 hours off, seven days a week. When they finished work they liked to relax and have a little entertainment, Mick explained, without elaborating any further.

That first night at the base I started to get to grips with how things worked around there and to find out exactly what Mick had meant by 'entertainment'. When off-duty, the Aussie miners seemed to spend the majority of their time in the bar, entertaining an assortment of local ladies who seemed to be a permanent fixture around there – the same sort of women, it has to be said, as I'd seen in the hotel in Bamako.

After chatting with the bartender, I discovered that some of the drillers on the site would pick up a sex worker in Mali, before they travelled down to the mine. The deal was they paid the working girls to accompany them for the entire time they were there – so often for several months on end. It meant there were always guys in the bar on the piss and a woman or two on the bar dancing. Whenever a driller took his leave, he'd drive his woman back to Mali, before jetting off back to Oz, only to return for his next stint a few weeks later, when he would do it all over again.

Whatever floats your boat, I told the barman, wryly.

I was eager to get my head around how the company operated and what measures they had in place security-wise. I spent the next few days on the site meeting the workers and visiting the various drilling set-ups. It was a massive operation spread out across a ten-mile radius with twelve local villages dotted in between. Around 40,000 people lived in the area, a handful of whom were employed at the mine.

From the local staff I learned that ever since the Conakry football stadium massacre, the previous year, there had been increasing violence across the country, including an assassination attempt on the military leader, Moussa Camara, which had failed, leaving him clinging to power. With a presidential election planned for that June, the first since 1958, tension and unrest was spiralling ever upwards. Not surprisingly, Bullion Resources wanted an urgent provision in place whereby if violence erupted across the nation, and the roads back to Mali got blocked, there remained a safe route out for their employees.

I started carrying out recces of the local area to get a snapshot of things. One of the best adages I'd learned in the military was the Seven Ps: Prior Planning and Preparation Prevents Piss-Poor Performance. It had saved my skin many a time. Here in the Siguiri mine it was crystal clear that when the time came to get the hell out of Dodge – as I was sure it would do – running through the Seven Ps now would pay off big time.

I began working my way through the obvious questions the Seven Ps threw up. How many soldiers are in the vicinity and how many police? Is either force in any sense reliable? Who are the people in the local villages – one tribe or many tribes, and what are the inter-tribal rivalries? How many locals are on the company compound? Are they all from the same area or tribe? What was the scale of displacement into the area from neighbouring countries – what scale of a refugee problem did we have here? Are the refugees being drawn to the mine itself? If so, why? What is their mindset? Are they happy, content, or are they unruly? What's the general mood of the place?

Changes in mood and atmosphere in a potentially hostile area are key indicators that something is afoot. In a country like Guinea and a region such as this, I needed eyes and ears in as many places as possible.

In the midst of going through the Seven Ps, I met up with Peter du Toit, a guy who worked for a South African company. He was employed solely to change the tyres on the massive trucks operating at the mine. He told me it was a two-day job just to change the one tyre. Judging by the size of them, I didn't doubt it. More importantly, the company he worked for were independent of Bullion Resources, and I figured he'd offer an unbiased perspective on things. He was likely to see stuff that I wouldn't see, and to talk about stuff Bullion Resources employees might feel they shouldn't say. He'd certainly know if there had been any accidents with the trucks, or a shutdown on any of the roads due to civil unrest or otherwise. Equally, he'd know if there was any unrest amongst the drivers that could indicate trouble further down the line.

As with so much of my life in the military, I was spending a vast amount of time collecting and collating intelligence – gathering and sorting the most valuable information. But every bit as important was building up a network of contacts who might prove useful if you found yourself in the shit – like in the midst of a civil uprising in war-torn Africa. Basically, it all comes back to the 'hearts-and-minds' type work, something the SAS pioneered in the Second World War, and which has proved so vital in numerous military campaigns ever since. Firepower has its place, but winning people's trust and gaining their support can often secure far more in war than the fiercest of battles.

From Peter I learned that the main breeding ground for unrest at the mine was the local villages, few of which felt the mining operation benefitted them much, if at all. If I was to start trying to win the battle for hearts and minds, that was where I should target my initial efforts.

I started probing the villages nearest to the gold mine, looking for those that might be most receptive. The first thing that struck me was that they were all jam-packed full of kids. The second thing that struck me was that the kids were playing street football with just the bare minimum of kit. It was clear they hadn't got a clue about team-work or even the rules of the game: it was just a chaotic, mad free-for-all as they battled for possession of a scrappy tennis ball they'd no doubt scavenged from some rubbish tip.

I've always loved football. To me it's one of life's great levellers, breaking down barriers in a way that nothing else can. When I saw those kids, I felt sure I could forge a common bond with them, one that would hopefully bring their parents and the village elders on-side. Bullion Resources had a few bits of footie kit and some footballs knocking about, so I figured it wouldn't be long before I'd have 'Mr Phil's Football School' up and running. That, most crucially, would be my Trojan horse – my way into their hearts and minds.

Footie would also provide the perfect excuse to do a spot of in-depth reconnaissance. I know that as soon as I start playing football with them, word will spread; the kids will tell their mates and their families, and before long the village elders will all want to come and see what was going on at Mr Phil's Football School. It offers me a chance to get in with the locals, to build up good relationships and hopefully to be seen as one of the good guys. Footie – in my book, there's no better way to get right into the locals' heads and their hearts.

My aim here is simple: when things start to go horribly wrong in the midst of a nation-wide uprising, we will drive the mining staff out through those villages who have signed up to Mr Phil's Football School, wherein everyone remains friendly – at least, towards us. That will offer us a safe route out. While their mates are starting to drag out the AK-47s from under their beds, we'll be nodding and smiling as our footie team buddies wave us through.

It sounds overly-simple, but that's pretty much how it works the world over. I've seen it countless times – in Gaza, in Afghanistan and in Iraq, footie-based hearts-and-minds activities have got me out of any number of tight spots. Although there's an overriding operational purpose to what I'll be doing here in Guinea with the football, it doesn't mean that we can't have some fun along the way.

Yet nothing is ever quite as straightforward – or as safe – as it seems.

CHAPTER ELEVEN

HIGH TEA WITH THE CROCODILES

Before I can make much of a start on Mr Phil's Football School, Mick makes it clear there are other priorities for me too. Alongside the reconnaissance of the immediate mining area, he tells me Bullion Resources is desperate for me to carry out a series of risk assessments on the residences of their senior employees and their investors. The company wants reassurances that in the event of the worst kind of unrest, they will be secure in their homes, or at worst, if they have to leave, they can be given safe and speedy passage out of the country.

Together, Mick and I set off shortly after sunrise, heading for Conakry, the capital of Guinea, situated on the coast. Home to Bullion Resources' regional headquarters and staff, it's also where some of the wealthy private investors who are financing the mining operations have their residences.

These are the 'big cheeses' that I've got to ensure can be safely evacuated, should it all go pear-shaped. It can take as long as fourteen hours to drive from Siguiri to Conakry, on roads riddled with chaotic and unpredictable checkpoints. We've managed to get Andy Smith, a fellow private security contractor, to accompany us for this stage of proceedings, as we expect trouble will be lurking somewhere up ahead on the long road to the capital. Andy's a solid, highly-experienced operator and a fine wingman – it's great to have him along.

We make as much progress as we can in the relative cool of the early morning, before checkpoint tempers really start to fray. As is so often the case, corruption and extortion are rife. The endless series of roadblocks lining the main roads are there for one thing only: to extract money out of travellers. Anyone not complying – paying the bribes – faces lengthy and unpredictable documentation checks, and quite possibly a spell locked up in a shipping container, to fry.

The miles flit by, but eventually we drive into the haze of a dusty, sun-blasted, blistering-hot afternoon. Shortly, I'm to get my first taste of the drug-addled child soldiers here – the shock troops manning the road-blocks somewhere up ahead.

With all the armed strife spilling over from neighbouring countries, some 7,000 young men, many just kids, have volunteered to form a civilian militia to support the Guinean army. Many have turned their new-found 'military' skills into a means to survive, setting up roadblocks to stop and loot vehicles. For anyone growing up in a country that – despite its mineral wealth – has one of the lowest standards of living in Africa, the chance to make money by whatever means is a temptation too great to resist.

Easy to control and manipulate and often utterly fearless, many of the teenage kids have been coerced into soldiering by their older peers, and fed drugs like marijuana, crack cocaine or amphetamines to numb their emotions and to enable them to detach themselves from reality. All of this poses a very real danger for the likes of Mick and myself, as we try to execute a drive from one side of the country to the other.

It's shortly before 2.00 pm when we approach a particularly dodgy-looking checkpoint, the sun blazing down from a furnace-like sky. I'm eyeing the two kids standing there. Neither of them looks much older than thirteen, and each is weighed down by the distinctive form of an AK-47 assault rifle. As we draw closer, I can see they have the glazed-eye look that indicates they're either high as kites on drugs, or drunk on whatever home-made hooch they've got their hands on. Most likely a bit of both.

We've been warned to do whatever we have to do to get through. I buzz down my window and try to strike up whatever conversation I can, while giving my best winning smile. It gets me absolutely nowhere. Without warning the smaller of the two kids grabs his AK-47 and within seconds he's shoved the barrel through the open window right into my face. I can feel the sun-warmed steel of the muzzle digging into my cheekbone, as he begins to fire all kinds of questions at me in broken English.

His breath reeks of alcohol, but from the bloodshot redness of his eyes and the massive size of his pupils, I figure he's on a lot more than just a shot of the local hooch. I get the sense of the main thrust of his questions: he's demanding to know where we're going and if we have the right 'papers' to allow us to proceed. I try to remind myself that he's still just a kid, and to keep my cool. As calmly as I can I tell him we're heading down to Conakry on a spot of mining business. More questions are fired at us, and no matter what kind of answers are proffered the muzzle of the kid's AK remains firmly jammed up my nostril.

It's then that I spot his T-shirt with a tatty old Adidas label on it. I try to zone in on the brand, hoping that he's a football fan or at least has some interest in the sport. But when I start banging on about all the Premier League teams he surely must have heard of, he doesn't seem to understand a word. No matter what players I swear blind are my best mates 'back in England', the gun muzzle remains firmly embedded in my face. We're getting nowhere fast, and Mick seems to have even less of a clue than I do as to what to do next.

It strikes me that there's no way I'm going to wrestle the AK47 out of the kid's hands, with a trigger-happy teenager as high as a kite standing at his shoulder. But it's then that I have a brainwave. I remember the bag of sweets I have in my jacket pocket. They're both still kids, after all, and what kid doesn't like a fistful of candy? Frankly, I'm ready to try anything right now. Reaching into my pocket, ever so slowly, so as not to get shot by the kid with his gun up my nose, I grab a handful of Jelly Babies and offer them to him. Incredibly, it seems to do the trick. Both he and his sidekick's eyes light up, as if all their Christmases have come at once.

Moments later the gun is withdrawn, as they start to wolf down the candies. It's not long before we're waived through. Unbelievable.

Mick and I were about to get slotted, or at the very least fried alive in a shipping container, and all for the price of a few Jelly Babies. There are a series of further checkpoints on the route to Conakry, at which we experience similar kind of treatment, but by now I've got the sweets at the ready. Amazingly, they seem to do the trick most times. Whenever they don't quite cut it, I pull

Left: At the exclusive Kingham Hill School, set in the leafy Cotswolds, aged around 13 years old. Sent there by the council, when I was in care, I quickly earned the nickname 'Council House Kevin'. Note the Anti-Nowhere League, punk band T-shirt, and how my right hand is flipping the bird. I did not fit in and I did not last long.

Left: By contrast I found my true calling in the British military – the first time I ever felt I really had a home. This is me in Londonderry, 1989, aged 19 years old, serving with the Royal Hampshires, packing an SA80 and feeling on top of the world.

Above: Myself, third from left of photo, with my army mates, Fas, Lee and Dave, in Kenya, where we were doing bush and desert training. Here we're necking a few Tusker beers in a local bar. Having just completed Army Commando training I'm proudly sporting a T-shirt that declares on the front: 'God Is Airborne' and on the rear 'He Failed The Commando Course.' I would go on to complete the Parachute Regiment's airborne training course myself, and to earn my own jump wings.

Above: While in Kenya we stopped off at the market stalls that line the road where it crosses the equator. This is me trying to convince a local trader that she should sell me this club for next to nothing. I got the stick for a price we both seemed happy with, so all's well that ends well.

Left: On guard at Nanyuki Showground, the British military's training facility, more formally known as BATUK (British Army Training Unit Kenya). You got a stick, not a gun, as they didn't deem the threat level high enough to warrant anything else.

Above: Snug in my hammock beneath my camouflage tarp, deep in the jungle. This is when me and my patrol deliberately got ourselves 'lost' so we might have a proper jungle survival experience, which was exactly what we did. And we loved every minute of it too.

Left: Myself in 2002, just after I had left the military to go on 'The Circuit' as it's called – the world of private military operations. I was 33 years old, and I had been posted to the Afghan capital, Kabul, to run a team of four guys with similar backgrounds to myself, plus 30-40 locals, protecting a European embassy and all its staff.

Above: More private security work followed, much of it in Africa. In Nigeria I trained the Presidential Guard Brigade, and in our down time myself and fellow operators did hearts and minds work – taking medical supplies and education materials around to local school and hospitals, and coaching the kids in football. Good local contacts can save your life in such situations. They did for me, many times over!

Left: In Israel myself and a fellow private security team took on what many viewed as a suicide job – often we were operating in the midst of the unrest, violence and rioting as seen here. But via our local contacts - and some inspired hearts and minds work - we managed to get the job done and get out alive.

Above: I'd stored up a whole world of trouble from my abusive childhood, and eventually the chickens came home to roost big time. Arrested for a 'domestic incident' I was jailed, as my life crashed and burned. By the time I got out, a family friend threw me a desperately-needed lifeline - labouring on a building site in London.

Right: With nowhere to live, a friend from my Army days offered me his abandoned caravan (pictured). It was green with mould inside and out, but I was desperate and I took it like a shot. I towed it to the London building site: home sweet home. It was from there that I stepped out each evening dressed in a £6.50 Paul Smith charity shop suit, trying to turn my life back around.

Left and below: I have made many mistakes in life, but my mantra is 'never give up.' I did turn my life around. I landed a role with Sky TV, making the hugely successful TV show called 'Fighting IS: Big Phil's War.' We went to Syria and Iraq, to film the war against ISIS from the viewpoint of an elite military veteran. Above, I'm pictured with a Russian PK machinegun – first used in 1961 – to show just how decrepit and ageing is the weaponry the Kurdish forces have to combat ISIS, which is a crying shame. Below, I'm with the Kurdish female fighters – the YPJ – outside of Al Hasakah, in Syria, on the front line. These women had had very little exposure in the media, and I was hugely privileged to be with them. These two showed me the enemy dead, to prove they were serious.

Left: In a Syrian refugee camp I filmed with the kids who'd been chased out of Al Hasakah by IS. I was truly humbled by the experience. Not one of those kids wasn't smiling, yet you cannot imagine what they had been through. They had seen far more horror than most people ever do in a lifetime. I learned so much from them.

Left: In 2016, all suited and booted, we - the Sky team – took the evidence we had filmed to the House of Commons, to garner support for getting more help and aid to the Kurdish fighters. I pushed the argument of how under-equipped the Kurds were and how, it they were fighting a war against IS on our behalf, then we needed to stump up and help them. It was the least we could do.

Above: Also in 2016 I joined SAS Who Dares Wins star and good pal Mark 'Billy' Billingham, on the London set of Ray Winstone's movie about an audacious London bank robbery. Billy was looking after Ray, just as I have body-guarded any number of high profile celebs in my time.

Left: In 2017 I organised and fought in the Remembrance Rumble, held in the York Hall in Bethnal Green, the home of British boxing. I'm pictured making my entrance for my fight against John Snyder, a former US marine and former professional boxer. I was 49 years old, we drew the fight and it was a great night. More to the point, we raised tens of thousands of pounds for services charities.

Above: In 2019 I was appointed the Army Cadet Champion, which is an immense honour, my role being to act as their ambassador. On the right I'm stood between Colonel Clinton Riley and Brigadier Mark Christie. I'm there to boost recruitment – getting people in both as adult volunteers and as young cadets, and aiming to turn them into better individuals in life, not just great soldiers. This remains a key focus and passion of mine today.

some insanely stupid faces to go with the Jelly Babies. I learn that as long as you make the kid-soldiers laugh, they'll let you through.

They are still just kids, after all. I think back to my worst times in care, when I was thirteen, fourteen and fifteen years old. I was a pretty violent and messed-up youth myself back then, and I doubt if I experienced anything like a fraction of what some of these young lads have suffered. Still, I realise I'm going to have to come armed with a sack-full of Jelly Babies – and a belly full of good humour – whenever we have to brave Guinea's highways.

We arrive in the capital by early evening. No one knows for sure how many people are crammed into Conakry, a sprawling city which itself is crammed onto a narrow spur of land jutting into the sea – the Kaloum Peninsula. Best estimates are in excess of two million, or one quarter of the entire population of the country. Power and water shortages are frequent, exacerbated by corruption and ageing machinery, plus the withdrawal of the French power company that partnered the government until 2007 (Guinea is a former French colony).

The downtown area is arranged on a grid system, forming a series of square blocks of buildings, intersected with highways, a little reminiscent of New York. It should make for ease of navigation and lessen congestion. Instead, it seems to do the opposite. The place is utter chaos. Those on foot seem to walk out straight into the traffic without so much as pausing to look, and those behind the wheel seem to live on their accelerators and their horns, stopping for no-one. The noise proves deafening.

But what strikes me most is the security ramifications of the city's basic grid-design: should any sort of uprising kick off, the military can close the place down in a heartbeat with a series of strategic checkpoints, taking control of the city in seconds. The resulting curfew would bring all movement to a standstill, blocking any escape, and there is of course no guarantee that the military in Guinea are the good guys. That means I need to find an alternative way out for all of the company staff and investors residing in the city, especially as Conakry is a bottleneck surrounded by sea on three sides.

We head to the residence of one of the most important individuals – a major investor in the Bullion Resources mining operations. Mr. Saul Rauf has lived in Africa most of his life and the company wants to ensure he's as safe as houses come any unrest: he's a key asset that they cannot afford to lose. He's evidently loaded by the looks of his Conakry villa, which is set back amidst extensive walled grounds, and surrounded by an immaculate series of lush tropical gardens.

Mick and I are ushered on to his patio, where we're served tea. Mr Rauf reminds me of how a classic old colonialist should look. He's tall, with an authoritative, upright posture and a vice-like handshake. Dressed in a dark-grey flannel suit, he's real old school, the sort that might say: 'If they won't stand still, then whip them.' Though he has distinctly Indian features, he's clearly lived in Africa for a very long time, and it seems he has picked up some of the quirky characteristics of a true West African, as I am shortly to discover.

As I sit there exchanging small talk and politely sipping my tea – and with various lackeys bustling about responding to Mr. Rauf's every whim – a swirl of movement in the nearby fish-pond catches my eye. Peering over the edge I am half expecting to see a few koi carp swimming around or even some goldfish. Instead, this long, pointed snout rises up through the water like a submarine coming to surface. In a flash the snout opens like a car bonnet, to reveal two jaws of razor-edged, glittering teeth. Before I can react, the jaws snap shut just as quickly as they opened, leaving two beady eyes locked onto mine.

In short, Mr Rauf's fish-pond is actually home to crocodiles, and these aren't your dwarf variety either, but the big old full-sized critters.

I settle back to have another sip of my tea, making a mental note to keep a good distance from the Mr Rauf's croc-pond. Perhaps sensing my surprise, Mr Rauf hauls out a big metal bucket from behind his chair, plonks it down in front of us and proceeds to grab a very pink and very raw-looking chicken – the sort you'd see in the chiller cabinet at Tesco's. Without further ado, he lobs the chicken over his shoulder, its trajectory taking it in the direction of the croc-pond. But not quite far enough . . .

It lands with a hollow, featherless, sickly plop on the edge of Mr. Rauf's patio, the one on which we're politely sipping our tea. Moments later the nearest croc hauls itself out of the water, scuttles forward, its claws clacking across the patio tiles as it does so, and then with an almighty snap its jaws open and it swallows the chicken in one go. In case we didn't get a proper eye-full the first time, we get an action replay. Mr Rauf grabs the remaining chicken from the bucket and lobs it in the direction of another of the crocs. Just like before, it hauls itself onto the patio and there's a big toothy snap and the chicken is kaput.

Mick and I exchange glances. I can't quite stifle the belly laugh that's burbling up from deep within. I feel like I've been parachuted into the set of a James Bond movie, with Mr Rauf as the arch villain, thought instead of stroking a fat white long-haired cat, he chucks dead chickens to crocodiles. In fact, Mr. Rauf out-Bond's any Bond villain I've ever seen. It's totally surreal and quite insane – but when all's said and done you have to see the funny side.

I figure that's what Mr. Rauf's about, too. As far as he's concerned, there's little point taking any security advice from white guys like us, if we can't handle the odd close encounter with a crocodile. This is a test. If we're frazzled by his croc-show, we're clearly not up to task – especially not in this part of the world. Conversely, if we can take it all on the chin – and see the funny side – we're maybe worth listening to. Perversely, this is hearts-and-minds stuff too, just at the opposite end of the spectrum from your average African villager.

I'm wondering what other bizarre and crazed goings-on Mr Rauf's got cooking behind the scenes in this rather splendid villa. Tea-drinking and croc-feeding done for now, I take a proper gander around and the place is mostly about as secure as can be expected. I make some recommendations, including clearing the vegetation from his border fences and walls, erecting some better security lighting and installing some extra CCTV, before cracking a joke that another crocodile in the pond wouldn't go amiss, to help keep guard.

For a moment Mr. Rauf's features remain utterly stiff and rigid, as if the joke has landed in very bad taste. I wonder if now is the time that Mr. Phil gets fed to the crocs, but I've always believed that if you're gonna be a bear, be a grizzly. I tend to speak my mind.

After a few, decidedly tense, seconds Mr. Rauf's features crack and he's all smiles. He agrees that another croc to fend off any would-be bandits would be no bad thing. We part on the best of terms, Mr. Rauf inviting us to join him for dinner during our time in Conakry. His parting shot is to let us know what will be on the menu. No surprises – it's going to be chicken curry. But as matters transpire, we'll sadly have to decline Mr. Rauf's kind offer.

I've barely had time to sort an escape route for Mr. Rauf and his ilk – there's only one viable way out of the city, Conakry being built on a narrow peninsula, and that's via the sea – before Bullion Resources deliver a new set of instructions. I'm to fly back to the UK without delay, to present my findings and my security assessment to their risk management team, in their London headquarters.

I'm more than a little saddened to miss out on Mr. Rauf's dinner invitation and doubtless some further croc-related high jinks, but I dutifully pack my bags and head for home.

Some twenty-four hours later I touch down at Heathrow and head directly to the firm's plush SW1 offices, feeling more than a little dislocated and all at sea. Needless to say, Knightsbridge is a whole world away from Checkpoint Alley, Jelly-Baby-addicted child soldiers and Mr. Rauf's crocodile pond. Regardless, as best I can I proceed to brief Bullion Resources' risk analysis team on what's what in Guinea. Mostly, they're desperate to learn what I make of the stability in the country – or rather, the lack of it – and how in the lead-up to the elections things are likely to change.

I give it to them straight. The truth is, no one can predict with one hundred per cent certainty exactly when or how civil unrest will present itself, but there are always the 'combat indicators' – changes in the local environment and especially in people's behaviour that are the early signs that trouble is brewing big time. I tell them that I think the country is horrendously volatile, but that with the right preparations their people can be safely extracted– both from Conakry and from the mine site – should things turn ugly.

I outline my strategies – and the costs involved – and there are barely any quibbles. They want me to get myself back out to Guinea pronto and to get it all sorted. I tell them I'm happy to do an about-turn, but there are two conditions. First, I need another person with me to operate effectively, and as back up, if the situation escalates. Second, I need a budget to fund my footie-related hearts-and-minds operations with the locals. Without batting an eyelid they agree: I'm given the go-ahead to hire someone of my own choosing, and to purchase all the football kit I can carry.

I ring around some of my former elite military muckers. Predictably enough, a lot of the blokes are busy, but luckily I manage to strike gold: I secure the services of my good mate Jim Munro, a former SAS trooper, a top man and a fantastic operator. As a bonus, Jim's already in-country, so he's well-acclimatised to operations there. He'll be a great asset for carrying out further recces, and I feel sure we'll be heading down to Conakry sometime sooner or later, and Jim knows the lie of the land there pretty damn well.

Jim's a lithe, sinewy sort of guy who's got the ability to rough it in the worst of environments, while also being able to pass muster with the higher echelons of society, the Mr. Rauf's of this world included. He is red hot with vehicles and road moves or navigating off-road terrain. That makes him perfect for the Guinea job, and he's also a skilled medic, which I sense is going to come in handy somewhere down the line.

Operating solo is all well and good when the situation is tightly contained, but the job in Guinea is far from being that. It presents as a fast-moving, volatile situation, requiring a variety of disciplines to deal with it. A second pair of hands and an additional clear head will prove indispensable where we're going. In the military we always worked in pairs – that was the smallest operational unit you'd ever deploy in. The golden rule was: never alone, or not if you could help it. At its simplest, you always need someone to cover your back no matter what the situation. Besides, for some of the strategies I have in mind for Guinea, two pairs of hands are definitely required.

Twenty-four hours later I'm at Heathrow, about to catch a flight. Before boarding the aircraft, I stock up on all the Jelly Babies I can lay my hands on. After an overnight in Bamako, I head across the border into Guinea, down to the mines in Siguiri and on to the camp. I rendezvous with Jim, and we figure one of our first priorities is to build up detailed maps of the whole area surrounding the mine.

We start to drive cross-country, up into the mountains and over these vast, featureless desert plains, looking for routes that will take us back across the border into Mali, while avoiding all roads and what they inevitably bring – checkpoints. We stay off-road and avoid all human settlements, looking for remote-area escape routes in case things turn bad. Every evening we return to the mine site with a little more intelligence, and bit-by-bit we start piecing it all together. It's painstaking work and it could all be for nothing.

But something – some sixth sense – tells me that at this moment in Guinea's history, it's going to prove a total life-saver.

CHAPTER TWELVE

MR PHIL'S FOOTBALL SCHOOL

One of the main priorities is to launch into the programme for Mr Phil's Football School, encompassing all twelve villages that surrounded the mine. But before Jim and I can really get started, there's an emergency on the outskirts of the mine camp itself. I'm well aware that there's a huge and illegal 'miners' village' that's been established on the fringes of the main slag heap. The place is literally an accident waiting to happen.

I've had it earmarked as somewhere we've got to check out, for it's got to be a source of local unrest. Before we can do so, disaster strikes. The mine operates by extracting all the earth from a site identified as being rich in gold, and transporting it in the giant trucks to a separate location where it can be processed and the ore itself extracted. The remaining dirt is then loaded onto other trucks and dumped onto a series of enormous slag heaps. It's there that the illegal miners start their digging. The key problem, of course, is that the slag heaps are not in any sense conventional mining terrain: they're just vast unstable piles of earth that haven't even started to properly settle. So, the illegal miners aren't digging into any sort of firm ground, but into an insecure mountain of dirt, which is little short of a death trap.

Regardless, extreme poverty drives people to take extreme risks. Many of the locals are so desperate they'll put their lives on the line for the chance of finding a tiny nugget of gold. One morning shortly after our return, Jim and I hear that the inevitable has happened: one of the slag heap mines has collapsed. We head out to see what we can do to help and to assess the risk. The minute we lay eyes on the scene we both realise there is zero chance for any of the men inside: they are all very, very dead.

Outside of the hole that they've tunnelled into the side of the slag heap we count thirty-odd sets of shoes and flip-flops. They've been left there by the men before they entered the tunnel, for they prefer to do the mining barefoot. It's a clear indication of just how many people have lost their lives, especially as the line of footwear is no longer at a tunnel entrance: it's at what was the entrance to a now fully-caved-in tunnel.

Word of the catastrophe has spread like wildfire, and already there are scores of women and men wailing in despair, clawing at the dirt with their bare hands and tearing their hair out. More and more distraught figures are turning up by the second. Jim and I realise there's nothing we can do – it's too late for saving any lives. Crushed under thousands of tonnes of slag, the illegal miners will have died instantly, or if not they will have suffocated to death. If we hang around any longer, the families will doubtless look to us to do something, but sadly there is no resurrecting the dead. There's not even a chance of retrieving any of the bodies. All we can do is make our exit as quickly and as discreetly as possible.

Clearly, the slag heap is a flash-point for trouble. Such tragedy will breed resentment and that will fester. I make a mental note to raise it as an issue, not that I can see exactly how the mining company can address it. No matter how they try to secure the slagheaps, no amount of fencing or walls will keep out a bunch of determined – illegal – miners. The lure of the gold will just keep sucking people in again.

The risks of such ever-present flashpoints underline the need for viable escape routes. Jim and I start to cut around the villages, seeking out any navigable dirt tracks that avoid the checkpoints on the main roads. As we do so, we witness one traffic accident after another. The roads are dire here in Guinea, the driving standards non-existent and most vehicles wouldn't be considered road-worthy anywhere in Europe – it's a recipe for disaster. We tend to moan in Britain about potholes, but the size and depth of the craters in Guinea mean if you end up being swallowed by one, you're unlikely to get out – not unless someone offers you a tow or a push.

As we dash from village to village, mapping out possible routes of escape, I'm itching to pick up where I left off with the football training. As I chat to Jim about it, he comes up with a cunning plan, one designed to complement Mr. Phil's Football School. Jim figures we should present ourselves as aid workers, for he has the medical training to help treat any number of ailments. Coupled with my football nous, it means we can offer a simple service in all of the villages – checking the kids for fleas and offering basic first aid, with the added bonus of some footie training and kit thrown in.

Jim will be the medic and I'll be the sports guy. It's a wrap-around service, and we can offer it all under the umbrella of the mine's 'community outreach work'. It offers the perfect disguise, to ensure we don't come across as being what we really are – security professionals. Of course, if our true reason for being there is discovered, we'll be well and truly stuffed and probably roasted on one of the village fires. Security just isn't something anyone will take kindly too, and especially if delivered under the guise of community work. Plus any trust we'll have built up will be well and truly blown.

But we both figure that is a risk well worth the taking.

We gather up some of the football strips, plus balls, and head down to the nearest village. I can see the same few kids playing with their scrappy tennis ball, and I figure it's high time they get a taste of what the real game is all about. As a teenager I'd hoped to trial for Southampton Football Club – I grew up in that area – and one or two of the coaches had figured I had the gift. It had all gone pear-shaped when the abuse had reared its ugly head, forcing me further off the rails. It was going into the Army that proved the saving of me – otherwise, I've no doubt I'd have ended up in prison.

Jim and I pull over and start to unload the kit, which results in a crowd gathering thick and fast. The kids have their eyes out on stalks. I do a head count and there are ten of the regular players from the village. It's not exactly a full squad, but enough to split them into two teams of five. French is the official language in Guinea, a legacy of colonial rule. My specialist language in the military was Spanish, in which I am pretty fluent. But via a smattering of schoolboy French, hand gestures and pidgin English I manage to make myself understood, and the kids seem more than up for a game.

I lay out a temporary pitch on a bit of wasteland, mark out the corners and get them doing some simple warm-up exercises and drills. The kids here are long-limbed and athletic and it's clear they've got good coordination, but after a couple of minutes of getting them to follow a few basic drills they're all off doing their own thing again. Setting an example, Jim and I try to get them to pass the ball to one another, to engender a bit of team-spirit, but the tallest lad, a kid called Sekou, keeps dashing off with the ball whenever it comes his way. No matter how often I repeat the simplest of drills they're all over the place. I realise I'd have more luck herding cats.

Regardless, we select two teams and decide to just get stuck in, hoping they'll begin to understand that football is a game of teamwork and everyone has their role. But it's hopeless. Everyone in Africa is a centre forward, or so it seems. I attempt to show one of them how to head a ball, and then they're all insisting they're the one to head the ball into the goal. Still, you can't fault their enthusiasm or their fitness or their willingness to have a go! More to the point, we're having a real laugh, even if they are running around the pitch like lunatics trying to steal the ball off each other the whole time.

Our performance hasn't gone unnoticed, either. Out of the corner of my eye I see a couple of the adults appear out of the huts. They stand and stare for a while. No doubt, this is a rare sight, a couple of the mine workers – who else could we be? – playing football with the village kids, and providing all sorts of fancy footie kit as well. Finally, they amble over to have a few words. I explain what Jim and I are about and suggest that maybe we'll get some of the adults to join in? They can even become assistant coaches in Mr. Phil's Football School. The seed has been planted and this is a fine start to our hearts-and-minds operation.

Jim and I call it a day, giving the team captains a football each and telling them we'll be back tomorrow for some more of the same. The reaction of the boys is one of total ecstasy – they start whooping and dancing about wildly, as they all seem to take up the same, spontaneous chant: 'Toubabou Phil! Toubabou Phil! Toubabou Phil!'

What the hell is that about, I wonder? I ask one of the adults. He smiles, a little sheepishly. 'Toubabou' has various meanings, he explains. It can refer to a 'wealthy traveller' or even a 'missionary', but when used by the village boys in this context it means simply 'white man.' It is not meant unpleasantly, he hastens to add.

White-man Phil. Hmmmm . . . I figure I may as well roll with the punches. Around here, I have a feeling it's going to stick.

For the next week or so Jim and I concentrate on building the reach and profile of Toubabou Phil's Football School. (It makes sense to change the name to something that will stick with the locals . . .) Jim gets right into his bush medic act, treating all kinds of ailments, while I get busy handing out football kits, plus advice and training to the kids. But it proves far from easy or straightforward.

I discover I only have to be suspected of giving a little bit of extra training to one team, and to be favouring that village, for the others to start shouting and gesticulating that they want exactly the same. There's a huge rivalry going on between the various sides. While much of it is just the natural competition you'd get between any local footie clubs, Jim and I are starting to realise that with Guinea being a lot like one giant tinder-box, one wrong strike and the whole lot goes up in flames.

While we're operating under the pretext of hearts and minds, it could all so easily backfire. And one thing is for certain. There is no way we are ever going to get any of the kids to gel as a team, no matter what village they may be from. Like I say, everyone's a centre forward in Africa.

By the end of that first week Jim and I have recce'd all the local villages, and made good headway in planning our routes out, not to mention recruiting friendly footie teams along the way. What we need to do now is to check on those Bullion Resources staff and key personnel living further afield, and especially those based down Conakry way, where I need to get an update on whether my maritime escape strategy has been properly acted upon.

As we start the drive south towards the capital, Jim and I sense fairly quickly that things have changed. The main road is thronged with child soldiers, and they're bunched up at every checkpoint. Jelly Babies no longer seem to cut the mustard. Jim and I are forced to hand over a good few fistfuls of one-dollar bills, to ease our way through. It's always good to carry a wad of small-denomination US dollars when travelling in Africa, for just such eventualities.

In that way we avoid the worst of the confrontations, but still Jim and I suffer the odd AK47 muzzle jammed up our nostrils. It strikes me that the kids doing the muzzle-shoving are no different really from those attending Toubabou Phil's Football School. That's the tragedy of this part of Africa. Kids like this hit a crossroads at such an early age, one from which there isn't much of a chance of turning back: hang out in the village and kick around a ball, or sign up as a child soldier. It's brutal.

Though we manage to avoid the worst of it, the level of tension and violence has escalated noticeably. We come across some seriously murderous road accidents. At one stage a truck has tried overtaking on a blind bend and ploughed into a mini-bus coming the other way. As we crawl past the twisted and bent carcass of the mini-bus, it's total and bloody carnage. A little further on another speeding trucker has failed to stop at a checkpoint. The militia have chased him down and dragged him from his cab. As we drive past trying to avoid their notice, we can see the worst of the check-point thugs laying into the poor guy, giving him a beating he will be lucky to walk away from.

By the time we hit the outskirts of Conakry, my mind is clear: trouble is brewing in Guinea, and I figure it's not long now before it will boil over into wholescale massive violence. Mick, Bullion Resources' liaison with us, had warned us before departing that Guinea's intelligence services have been working overtime of late. Sensing impending trouble, they have upped their surveillance on anyone travelling to and from the mines – the nation's main source of wealth.

Of course, with Guinea being under one kind of authoritarian rule or another for decades, any trust that may have existed between the state and its citizens has been eroded. It's left a constant underlying tension in its place. Suspicion – maybe even hostility – towards strangers is a corollary to that, and especially in a nation that has only known one way of life for so long. In such a country ruled by such a system, the elite are to be resented and mistrusted, for they have only ever looked out for their own. We *toubabous* aren't a great deal different – we're just a wealthy elite coming in from the outside.

The changes brought about by the mining industry are significant, no doubt about it. But to the masses, raw resources extraction has just meant more money for those in power, and a widening gap between the haves and the have-nots. For a country where unrest and discontent fester and grow quickly, violence is never far away. That's what the nation's intelligence services are on high alert for now. And from Mick's warning, it's clear that on our arrival in Conakry there may well be a reception party waiting for us.

There's really only one decent hotel in Conakry – the Grand. We've agreed to meet an associate of Bullion Resources there, to discuss security for the mine during the upcoming elections – the million-dollar question right now. We pull onto the main freeway, the Autoroute Fidel Castro, that leads down into the city centre, and we're into the heart of typical West African chaos. Crowds of people mill about in the middle of the road, motorcycles cut in and out of the cars and the pedestrians, and drivers just stop wherever they feel like it, oblivious to the fact that there's a truck right up their rear. Somehow, a guy cycles calmly through the lot, with one hand on his handlebars and a fridge balanced on his head. Cycling. With a fridge. Balanced. On his head.

It strikes Jim and me as being a small miracle there aren't more smash ups. We negotiate the crazed lottery of a few of Conakry's bigger roundabouts, twisting and turning this way and that, when I clock this navy-blue saloon car that's sticking directly on our tail. I mention it to Jim and we decide to drive around a few more times, just to be sure. That confirms it: we have a tail. The guy was obviously waiting for us and must have been tipped off. For now, we keep to our planned rendezvous, knowing Mr. Blue Saloon Car will be following.

Our brand-new Land Cruiser 4x4 is hardly discreet. In fact, it's something of a giveaway that we've come from the mines. As Jim and I are both painfully aware, we stick out like the dog's nads amongst the battered and bashed-up Conakry traffic. The solution to this would be simple enough for the likes of Jim and myself: score a local vehicle and cut about making like locals. It's something I've done in many of the world's worst trouble spots – in Iraq, in the Gulf Arab states, in Afghanistan even.

In Kabul, I ran a security programme for a high-profile European embassy. My chosen mode of transport was a Kawasaki trials bike, which I'd ride dressed head to toe in an Afghan dishdash robe and wearing a pilfered Russian tankie's helmet – one that hailed from the time when the Soviet Red Army waged war in Afghanistan, which is accurately known as the 'graveyard of empires.' It was the kind of motorbike and dress any self-respecting local Afghan might favour. Plus the Kawasaki had the ability to cut through narrow alleys, along paths or up and down flights of steps, should the Afghans throw up unexpected roadblocks. I lost count of the times it got me out of trouble fast.

Here in Guinea, it may take some persuading to get Bullion Resources to allow us to eschew their fleet of flash vehicles, and bring in a battered, rusting, paint-peeling, sun-bleached Toyota Corolla instead. For now at least, we're stuck with the gleaming white Land Cruiser, which has barely a dent or a scratch upon it.

We pull into the Grand Hotel's entranceway, with Mr. Blue Saloon Car still hot on our tail. Here, the status conferred by the Land Cruiser is all too obvious. The hotel staff insist on opening our doors and fawning and scraping, presuming that Jim and I must have serious kind of money, to be driving such a vehicle. They're like flies around the proverbial honeypot. By contrast, Mr. Blue Saloon Car gets largely ignored, but not by the two of us.

We watch him pull in behind us, while trying to keep a discreet distance. A tall gangly bloke with a wispy moustache and massive dark glasses gets out and follows us into the hotel lobby. While we check in at reception, we can see him hovering, watching where we will go next. Jim and I have this meeting coming up, and we'd rather Mr. Blue Saloon Car doesn't get to overhear everything. We decide to head for the bar, positioning ourselves in an alcove in the far corner, where there is only the one table. At least this way Mr. Blue Saloon Car will find it hard to earwig our entire conversation. In fact, he'll have a real problem getting anywhere close to us.

With not a little eager anticipation, we sit with our backs to the wall and observe how Mr. Blue Saloon Car will handle himself. Predictably, he sits right opposite us – so as close as he can get, without joining us at our table. Keeping his massive shades on, he unfolds a newspaper and proceeds to busy himself perusing it, only every other second he's glancing across at the two of us over the top. His tradecraft is laughable. In fact, there's a part of me that is really starting to enjoy the situation.

Our guest, Mr. Bakri Omer, arrives and takes the proffered chair – which puts his back to Mr. Blue Saloon Car, making it even more difficult for him to clock what we're discussing. We order drinks and start to talk. Mr. Omer is a high-level business contact and friend of the mining company, who seems to know everything and everyone in Conakry. We're here for an exchange of information. Jim and I brief him on the security situation in the villages surrounding the mine. He briefs us on the all-important political developments in the capital.

Every now and then I steal a quick glance at our uninvited guest, who I've mentally nicknamed 'Inspector Clouseau'. Hiding behind his enormous newspaper, he keeps peering round the corners and over the top, as he tries to watch us like hawks. He's clearly been watching too many Pink Panther movies and I'm forced to stifle a chuckle.

Once we've finished with Mr. Omer – whose insight has proven seriously useful, confirming some of our worst fears – we escort him to the hotel lobby. Having seen him safely off, we return to the bar to pay the bill. It's then that I tell Jim that I think it's time we gave Conakry's Inspector Clouseau a run for his money. We make a move as if we're heading for the lobby area and he follows us like a dog. Once in the lobby I make a couple of dummy runs as if I'm about to leave, but change my mind at the last moment. As I do so, Conakry Clouseau literally jumps up and down trying to follow my every turn. Each time I walk out, he goes to follow, but then I walk back in again as if I've forgotten something and he's forced to sit back down again. I'm giving him a proper run around in the lobby and it's hysterical.

I'm doing this for a bit of light relief. It's tickling Jim and me something rotten. Whoever this geezer is he doesn't know the first thing about spying, laying low or even how to tail someone without being noticed. We're in need of the diversion and the laughs, after getting Mr. Omer's low-down. Basically, his take on things is that with political tensions mounting, it's only weeks now – maybe even days – before the whole country blows.

When we've had enough of torturing Conakry Clouseau, we leave the Grand with him trying his best to stay on our heels. Behind the wheel of the Land Cruiser once more, we're well on our way back up the Fidel Castro freeway, by the time we manage to lose him. We suspect it won't be the last we've seen of Conakry Clouseau, but we figured we'd try to shake him off, just to see how easy it was to do so. Just in case we may need to lose him for real at some stage down the line.

We head for the Bullion Resources office, to check that all is fine and dandy with our planned seaborne escape route from the city, should the likes of Mr. Rauf and Mr. Omer have need of it. Once we're satisfied that it is, we decide to drive back to the mine site directly. After Mr. Omer's warnings, Jim and I have a strong sense of urgency driving us forwards. It's clear where we'll need to be when – not if – things turn truly bad: at the mine, getting the Bullion Resources people safely out of there.

Here in Conakry, the sea offers the perfect close-at-hand get-away. At the mine, deep in-country, there is only one possible route out, and it involves complex navigation and highly-skilled driving across hundreds of miles of bush and desert terrain. Without Jim and I on hand, the mine staff will be stuffed.

Hence the decision to brave Guinea's roads, even though dusk will soon be upon us.

CHAPTER THIRTEEN

ESCAPE AND EVADE

We decide to drive the 500-mile stretch back in one go. As luck has it, we slip past the night-dark check-points without losing our liberty or our lives. We're a good few dollars lighter for the privilege, but we figure it's a small price to pay. Dawn is breaking by the time we reach the mining camp and we head straight for our accommodation huts. We're utterly exhausted after the long day on the road, and the half-dozen AK47 muzzles thrust in our faces, but something unexpected prevents us from crashing out right away.

Jim spots a lone figure slumped outside of one of the huts. We go to investigate and it turns out to be one of the Aussie drillers, who's had some kind of an accident. Though he's totally pissed, we get him to explain in a drunken slur what's happened. He's fallen over after a night boozing at the bar. He's in agony and he thinks he's hurt his leg.

Jim puts his medical training to use and checks the guy over. The right leg is clearly where the problem is: we can see his foot is at right angles to it, pointing ninety degrees in the wrong direction. Jim patches him up the best he can, but there's no question about it – the guy needs to be evacuated to a hospital. We alert the head office who arrange to have him cassevaced out of there.

The incident underlines one thing for us most powerfully: the expatriate staff live lives so disconnected from the reality of the country, they have zero idea of what's going on outside of the mine. Though Guinea is poised to blow, they're carrying on partying and getting pissed as newts, as if all was good with the world. It makes Jim and me wonder just what reaction we'll get when we announce that the time has come to haul ass out of there.

For the next few days we concentrate on nothing other than mapping out a series of alternative escape routes, ones which snake through the villages surrounding the mines – those that we've forged footie-friendly relations with. Crucially, each route isn't marked on any map but our own, they're utterly free of any checkpoints and so far off the beaten track even the locals have no use for them. And for this type of exit strategy, we definitely need wagons like the mining company's Land Cruisers: only top-notch 4x4s will stand any chance of getting through.

We build up a file with all the procedures that will need to be used in the event of an evacuation. We make sure we have a stack of Bergens packed for everyone, containing all the essentials for such a journey: food and water, warm clothing, navigational and survival aids, communications equipment. The idea is we can all just grab a pack and go, should we need to leave in a hurry. We also start to train key staff in the essential routines required to ensure all our people can get out quickly and safely. When all of that is sorted, Jim and I figure we've done all we can for now.

But make no mistake, everything has changed now – at least, once you step outside of the mine it has. Jim and I attempt a few more footie and medical liaison visits to the local villages, but each time we seem to have a Conakry Clouseau look-alikes glued to our tail. Maybe they have a place somewhere in Guinea where they clone these guys.

It's the run-up to the elections, and the streets of even the minor villages are crawling with men dressed in a raggedy assortment of uniforms. There are police, army and militia seemingly on every street corner, and it doesn't take a rocket scientist to work out that Guinea is a powder keg set to blow. There's a dark, seething atmosphere, and suspicion and unrest seem the order of the day everywhere we go. At each and every turn there are eyes watching. Scores of them, following our every move, dogging our every step.

To make matters worse, we learn that some of the local workers have failed to turn up at work and there have been serious confrontations on the front gate. It feels as if there's the beginning of a real shift in attitude towards the mining company, and the way I understand West Africa, any kind of disturbance in one place will spread, meaning there will be a displacement elsewhere. It's like a domino effect, and here the dominoes just never stop crashing down. Nothing ever calms down here much – the cause of all the strife just moves on to the next thing.

We learn that election campaigning has started in a nearby village, so we decide to go check it out. We head to an area where we've built up a good rapport over Tobabou Phil's Football School. But nothing seems the same anymore. Suddenly, not even the kids seem to want to talk to us. Just a few days back they were falling over themselves to accept our help. Now, there's a barely disguised sense of hostility in the air. In military-speak we'd use the phrase 'the weather's changed' – the temperature's suddenly gone from very sunny to very chilly, which means that we have to tread ultra-careful wherever we go now and whatever we decide to do.

Of course, on the positive side, this is proof that our hearts-and-minds campaign has worked – because we've got just the intelligence we needed. On the negative side, the escape routes we mapped through the 'friendly' footie villages might not be quite so friendly in the coming days.

The electioneering starts ramping up. We drive into a village where it's full-on carnival time. We have to slow the Land Cruiser to a crawl, as the crowds shout and cavort and dance across the street in wild disarray. Yellow banners are everywhere – which we know signify support for one of one of the candidates in the coming elections. In fact, the village is a sea of yellow from end to end. Drums are beating fast and strong and there's a frenzied atmosphere in the air.

Then we spot a figure who really takes the biscuit. He has painted himself from head to toe in bright yellow paint, including his face and his hair. The only thing he hasn't managed to turn yellow are his eyeballs and his teeth. He runs towards us as we edge through the crowd and seconds later he's flung himself onto the Land Cruisers' bonnet, landing with an audible thud, his arms and legs flailing about in abandon. I slam on the brakes, but he clings on for all he's worth, his face jammed against the windscreen, yelling and screaming out his support for the yellow party – whoever they may be.

Jim and I exchange glances. I can tell exactly what he's thinking: either this guy is totally off his face on something, or he's just checked out of the local lunatic asylum. I wholeheartedly agree.

As I've stopped the vehicle, Yellow Man seems to think there's no more fun to be had hijacking our ride. He peels himself off our car and proceeds to dance off down the street, leaving us none the wiser. We set off again, moving at a dead slow pace, clocking the surly-looking police and militia-men mingling with the crowds.

We reach the outskirts of the village, and suddenly a wild commotion blows up seemingly out of nowhere. At the edge of the road a crowd gathers around something prone on the ground. They are clearly agitated, the atmosphere explosive and febrile. We pull over to take a look. It turns out that there's a figure lying on the road, and he is the source of all their attention and their angst. As Jim and I try to make out who it is, we realise the figure is awash with yellow, from the ends of his hair to the tips of his toes. It is none other than Yellow Man, and everyone is crying out that Yellow Man is dead.

From what we can see they are absolutely right. Yellow Man is completely stone cold dead. Not only that, but somehow he's ended up lying there stark bollock naked. Neither Jim nor I can believe this is the same guy who took a fly-swat leap onto our windshield just twenty minutes earlier, being so crazy-full of beans. What on earth can have happened in the interim? Either way, neither of us need the brains of an archbishop to realise this is potentially very bad news. Yellow Man is dead – therefore someone has cursed the yellow candidate's fortunes in the coming election. That's how the locals will interpret it, as sure as eggs is eggs.

Sure enough figures start to shout and scream that the opposition party must have done this – that's the party standing against the yellow candidate's party. The cries go up that the opposition have cursed Yellow Man with a voodoo spell and killed him. No one seems to consider the possibility that Yellow Man may have died from lead poisoning, as he's lathered himself from head to toe in paint the colour of a canary, and it might just be toxic.

The jungle drums are beating well and proper, and scores of locals flock to the scene. We hear them take up the cries of anguish: *Yellow Man is dead! The opposition have killed him! Their voodoo is to blame!* The road is filling up with a jostling, agitated crowd and soon our escape route will be well and truly blocked. It only takes one person to decide that Yellow Man has actually fallen victim to the white man's juju, and Jim and I are going to face a lynching.

We make a swift exit in the Land Cruiser, getting the hell out of there while we still can. But if it's this bad up-country, what is it like in the capital, we wonder? We decide to risk what we figure will be a final road trip south, to gauge the capital's temperature. Close to boiling point is an understatement. On every corner of the city there are phalanxes of soldiers tooled up to the nines, brandishing assault rifles, bandoliers of ammo, grenade launchers and invariably boasting the back-up of a technical – a 4 x 4 pickup with a heavy machine gun mounted on its rear.

Many sport the distinctive red berets, which signify they're either from the Autonomous Presidential Security Battalion – more commonly known as the Presidential Guard – or from Guinea's Airborne Battalion, who style themselves as the nation's airborne commandos. Either way, ever since the coup there's been an upsurge in acts of extortion, thievery and violence by these very same forces, not to mention rape. In short, having these guys roaming the city streets is a little like having the lunatics take control of the asylum.

Jim and I don't linger long. No more than a couple of hours. It's all we need to convince ourselves to listen to our gut instincts, which right now are screaming that we need to get the hell out of Guinea. We head back to the mine and report all that we've seen. We get the green light to do what is the only sensible option right now – to organise an immediate evacuation of all non-essential staff.

We get a dozen or so – mostly the Aussie drillers – in the vehicles as quick as we can and send them straight down the road to Bamako, Mali, and well away from any danger. Jim and I and the remaining expatriates number less than half a dozen now. We figure we'll hold on for a few days more, just in case we've called it wrong. But as we feared, the election has stirred up huge unrest among the villages, and it's about to spill over in our direction.

That evening, we hear of an incident on one of the roads. A speeding truck has hit and badly injured one of the locals. It's not one of the mining company's vehicles, but there's no convincing anyone of that. Overnight, the villagers get themselves worked up into believing it was one of our trucks, and we get the sense that emotions are at boiling point.

At first light one of the few remaining admin staff comes running into my hut, asking me to hurry to the front gate. Wondering what on earth can have happened now, I tear over there, only to discover a group of several dozen angry men and women laying siege to the gate and yelling at the mine staff. Predictably, they've brought the accusation that the speeding truck was a mining truck to the gates of the mine. It's total bullshit, but the rumour mill is churning and it's ended with a rent-a-mob on our doorstep. As tempers boil over the first rocks are thrown and I can see it turning very, very ugly.

I've got that tingling sensation running up and down my spine. I know exactly what it means whenever I feel it. *Danger, big time.* Something is about to go horribly wrong . . . unless Mr. Phil can somehow defuse the situation a little. I look around for Jim, but he's nowhere to be seen. No reason he should be up and about, as its barely dawn. I have that gut-wrenching feeling that things are poised to explode.

Needs must. Time to step into the fray.

I move out in front of the gate to speak with the ring-leaders. I'm more vulnerable here, but I'm also reaching out to them in the hope that it will make a real difference. Big risk – potentially big pay back if I can bring the tension levels down a notch or two. I repeat the line we've been using ever since the accident: no one from the mine had the slightest bit to do with it. But I offer to drive out and investigate and see what Jim and I can do to help – Jim being a medic and all.

Fortunately, one or two of those in the crowd recognise me from Toubabou Phil's Football School. It turns out they've also heard about Jim's medical work. It's now that our hearts-and-minds programme really starts to pay dividends. They intercede on my behalf, convincing the ring-leaders that Mr. Tobabou is indeed a man of his word.

Grumbling, seething, gradually the crowd at the gate dissipates. It's a reprieve, but I feel sure it won't last for long. I go fetch Jim and we drive out to take a look for the road traffic accident victim. En route, we see more signs of the strife and the trouble that is sweeping the area. We pass the local airport – no more than a tiny dirt strip carved out of the bush – and spy the smouldering wreckage of what is clearly a smashed-up aircraft. We learn from some of the locals that it was set alight by rioters last night, to stop it from taking off. No one quite seems to know why they did what they did, apart from that it's all to do with the election.

Oddly, I find it perversely reassuring. I'd ruled out the dirt strip as a way to get the staff out in an emergency, for the simple reason it's the clear and obvious point from which to try to execute a rapid evacuation. In other words, if the airstrip was our escape plan we would have all our eggs slap-bang in the one proverbial basket. All it would take is a mob like the one that destroyed this aircraft to get wise to our actions, and all would be kaput. Overland and off-road, there is an almost limitless choice of routes out of there. It's also a far less visible or predictable means of making an exit.

As Jim and I push ahead through the villages, we pass a horrendous pile-up. Apparently, two trucks have collided at speed, trying to avoid angry crowds of protesters. Protesting at what, we wonder? At Yellow Man's passing? Who knows? All we are sure of is that it's more fallout from the coming elections. We don't need to see any anymore.

We abandon our mission of mercy and head straight back to camp. We inform the head office and the few remaining staff that this is it – it's time to leave. All the effort Jim and I have spent rehearsing our off-road escape routes is now about to come into play, as we make our exit across the empty desert and savannah plains back towards Bamako.

The Bergens are all ready and waiting – our food, water and fuel rations safely stashed for exactly this moment. We source the best cross-terrain vehicles from the fleet of vehicles, and start rounding up the few remaining engineers and truckers. The only people we will leave here is a skeleton staff of locals, who will mothball the site for as long as we're gone. Our plan is to set off under the cover of darkness, come nightfall.

Of course, now we've made the decision to get the hell out of Dodge, the waiting is the worst thing, knowing that tensions are rising all around and at any moment we could have an angry mob back at the gates baying for our blood. But Jim and I are adamant: we cannot risk leaving without the cloak of darkness to conceal the direction in which we head. While we'll be off-road all the way, if anyone sees us leave they could set off after us, trying to trace our tyre tracks. You can only hide them in that sort of terrain by brushing them away with tree branches and the like, and that takes a great deal of time, which is a luxury we just don't have right now.

Just after sunset we get on our way in a small convoy of vehicles. As we hit the gas, we leave behind a trail of dust and little else, as our vehicles speed along the dirt tracks, taking a series of back roads. We've mapped every twist and turn, and we're more than happy to drive this route with lights out, navigating by the light of the stars and moon. Within thirty minutes we're well off the beaten track and away from any roads . . . or any checkpoints. In fact it's just us, open land, rolling hills and trees. Our journey will entail covering double the mileage of the route via the freeway, but we're pretty damn certain we'd be highly unlikely to make it out that way, without being stopped and detained, or possibly even killed.

For the next three hours our convoy drives non-stop. Jim and I have given strict instructions: no one risks getting out of the vehicles for anything or anyone, no matter what, until we know we're out of the country. It's about midnight when we cross the border into Mali, and in no time we hit the outskirts of Bamako. Fortunately, the hotel where this journey all began has enough rooms for the night, so Jim and I book everyone in. But before crashing out we join the Aussie engineers for a drink or two in the bar. After all that we've been through, it would be rude not to.

On one level, our flight out of Guinea feels like something of an anti-climax. Jim and I were all pumped up for action, but there was zero aggravation, violence or trouble of any sort along the way. I can tell that a few of the Aussie engineers are entertaining doubts: was it really as bad as we'd said it was out there? As the beers go down they start to give voice to their misgivings. By way of response I give it to them straight: tonight, we got out without hitting trouble and with no one losing their life *because* Jim and I had done our job so thoroughly. That's what we were hired for. That's why Bullion Resources called in the professionals. The fact we're all still at liberty and alive is testament to that fact that we've made our preparations exhaustively.

I remind the drunken Aussie drillers that Guinea is about to blow. Mark my words – any day now. And sure enough it does.

Shortly after our exit the run up to the elections is marked by violent clashes that sweep across the country, with large areas being placed under military lock-down. We made the right decision to get everyone out at exactly the right time. Any longer, and it could have proven fatal.

The morning after our escape from Guinea, Jim and I are sitting on the hotel veranda, tucking into a proper English breakfast, and some of the hotel's gorgeous French bread, as we muse over the last few months of madness. Toubabou Phil's Footie School; Conakry Clouseaus cloned by the thousand; Mr. Rauf's crocodile pond; stone-dead Yellow Man; stoned-out-of-their-brains child soldiers – we've survived it all unscathed. One thing's for sure – it's been an exhilarating, knife-edge ride.

The key thing is we got everybody out safely and without a single casualty. For Jim and me that's a job well done and we're glad to be heading home.

Until the next time . . .

CHAPTER FOURTEEN

REST IN PEACE

A very good friend of mine Rich, who runs a security company, owns this gorgeous house up in the wilds of the Welsh hills. He was out mowing his vast lawn one morning when he got chatting to his next-door neighbour who had recently moved in. As conversations go, Rich asked him what he did for a living and it turned out he was something to do with the Nigerian government's Office of the National Security Adviser, which does pretty much what is says on the tin. Rich's ears pricked up at the word 'security' – that was his line of work. He'd been taking teams of high-end security specialists in and out of Iraq over the years, and what Rich didn't know about security wasn't worth knowing.

The conversation moved to the subject of the security of Nigeria's then president, Goodluck Jonathan. Winning his first election fair and square in 2011, Goodluck had started his climb up the ladder ten years' earlier, when he'd taken over as governor in his home state of Bayelsa, after his boss was impeached on corruption charges. It seemed the fedora-wearing Goodluck was not only lucky by name but also lucky by nature.

Rich's neighbour revealed that the Office of the National Security Adviser were looking for a specialist team to train the Presidential

Guard Brigade, the elite unit of the Nigerian army. These were the personal bodyguards responsible for protecting the president of Nigeria, the first lady and other senior politicians. Never one to miss an opportunity, Rich jumped right in.

'Well, I can sure help you with that. My company offers just that sort of training. I've got a team of ex-special forces instructors who will get the president's men into shape in no time.'

From this rather bizarre conversation – from the back of a lawn mower, in Rich's case – Rich found himself jetting out to Nigeria's capital, Abuja, in the company of his Welsh Hills neighbour, to meet the Nigerian government. He received the gold-plated treatment and then some. At one of the government people's flash homes, someone cracked open a bottle of champagne with a gold golf club, and with the Moet flowing Rich managed to negotiate and secure a contract to train the Nigerian president's bodyguards . . . Truly insane.

Rich got to work setting up a training camp in an army barracks, not far from the capital Abuja. He sent a couple of Green Army lads out to begin the preparations for the first training course, but needed someone with an elite forces background to oversee the actual training.

He thinks of yours truly and calls me up to ask if I'm interested. You bet I am.

I pack my bags and fly off to Nnamdi Azikiwe International Airport, Abuja. Some decades back the capital of Nigeria used to be Lagos, but following an unprecedented population boom in the 1970's and 1980's, the government decided it was too polluted and overcrowded, so they built a brand-new city to keep the president safe – as you do – and far away from any coastal attacks. In 1991, Abuja became the nation's capital with the presidential villa and complex built around Aso Rock, a massive 400-metre monolith of granitic on the outskirts of the city.

As I'm driven along the shrubbery-lined highways, I realise how much planning has gone into building the city and I have to say it's pretty impressive. I arrive at the Hilton where I'm staying, along with the rest of the lads, and get a few Turbo King beers in before a good night's sleep and an early start the next morning.

The training camp for the president's men lies about 60 miles east of Abuja, in a pretty little town called Keffi. We're based in the officer's mess at the headquarters of 177 Guards Battalion, a proper Nigerian army unit. The 177 Guards Battalion's camp sits in extensive grounds, complete with immaculate lawns and manicured flower borders.

The team has pretty much got everything set up for the first bodyguard course, so when I arrive it's just a case of putting the final touches to the curriculum, to ensure it delivers more bang for their buck. The camp is a full-on place and a bit of a sweetshop for me and the team: they've got all the assets and equipment – classrooms, whiteboards and projectors, plus more importantly all the cars, weapons and ammunition you could wish for.

The first morning we hold an informal introduction in the classroom. I'm there with my white board and markers at the ready when in walk the students: twenty guys all dressed in black boiler suits ... and each carrying an AK47. As they proceed to sit down, their trusty weapons positioned in between their legs,

I'm tempted to point out that we're not on the shooting range yet and perhaps a pencil and a pad might be more appropriate. Still, I guess it shows they're keen, as long as it's not me they're using for target practice.

I've been told that they've been hand-picked from across the various regiments in the Nigerian military – the best of the best. But I'm wondering exactly who has done the selection. On first sight they're a mixed bag. Some are tall and athletic; others I doubt have seen the inside of a gym for a long while. Still they're here, and so am I, about to deliver my first full-blown bodyguard school for the Nigerian president's men. Surreal as it all may be, I'm determined to get them into the best shape possible.

We start off with the fundamental drills, moving on to the more advanced techniques, focusing on the specifics that I know they are going to need. At the end of the day, they're being employed to protect the lives of their country's leaders. This is close-protection work and requires an ability to respond instinctively to situations while employing a range of defensive measures. Being switched on one hundred per cent and staying alert to any potential threat is crucial, and it starts with situational awareness. Taking in the surroundings and assessing the dangers is among the first skills they'll need to master.

Looking at some of them dozing off, I know I've got my work cut out. I get them outside to wake them up a bit and to assess their physical strength and fitness. It doesn't take long to tell the difference between those who have seen combat for real, and those who have spent far too long behind the walls of the presidential villa. I doubt very much if they've tackled any assailants to the ground, let alone shot their gun for a good long while, judging by their reaction speed, or rather the lack of it.

After being with the trainees for a day, it's clear that not everyone is there because of their combatant skills or their competency as a soldier. A good few it seems have benefited from their relationship with those at the top. The fact that they're shite operators doesn't seem to matter.

Unfortunately, as I'm soon to discover, some are almost untrainable. No sooner have I explained the basics, than it's gone; in one ear and out the other. I find I'm having to watch two guys, Olu and Obe like a hawk the entire time. No matter how often I explain something very simply, they just don't understand and I know they never will. Most of the lads are fired up and engaged, but Olu and Obe are switched off like a blown lightbulb. I'm seriously wondering whether it's safe to hand them a gun let alone one that's fully loaded.

One of the first things I'm told by the officials paying for the course is that they need all of the soldiers to have a high standard of proficiency in weaponry, meaning they must be sharp-shooters. I guess that's why they turned up on the first day, guns at the ready. We head out to the back of the barracks where there's a ready-made firing range and I start to teach the lads the basics of live firing, before lining them up and preparing them for target practice. And boy do some of them need practice.

Olu and Obe, the classroom dozers, don't seem a great deal more awake in the open air. I have to stand behind them the whole time watching them like a mother hen with her chicks: God forbid they accidentally fire their weapon in the wrong direction, and kill themselves, some of the other trainees, or me. Fortunately, the rest seem sharp enough and while they might not all be naturals, they're at least paying attention.

We do loads of shooting from all different positions and by the time we've finished I feel, with a few exceptions, that the president and his men will be in far better hands. It comes as no great surprise that when we return to the classroom, Olu and Obe promptly fall asleep, leaving the rest of us to endure the rasping of their snores. It doesn't seem to matter to them what they may miss, because they figure they are guaranteed a place on the Presidential Guard, no matter what. Connections. It's all about connections.

Sure enough, despite my insistence that everyone should receive a pass or fail, I'm told in no uncertain terms by one of the officials that as we trainers are being paid to do a job, they will *all* pass with flying colours. End of. No discussions.

We're several days into the course when I decide to get the guys out and about in the vehicles. Driving defensively, and being able to shoot from vehicles and/or dismount and shoot are key close-protection drills. Essential. It's great to see the guys' enthusiasm and I'm beginning to hope my efforts are paying off. As close-protection officers, these guys will be accompanying their charges to a range of social events where they'll be in and out of vehicles like the proverbial yo-yo. Used properly, the vehicle should become their greatest defence against any assailant.

For much of my military life, the Seven P's have stood me in good stead and are still the foundation to everything military that I do: Prior Planning and Preparation Prevents Piss-Poor Performance. Without it you're a target before you've even got started. I need to instil in these guys that it's their job to limit or eradicate any opportunity for attack during any vehicle-based journeys. Preparation comes first; remaining alert and observant throughout second. But I suspect I'm going to have an uphill task with the sleeping beauties on the team.

The risk of an attack on the Nigerian president is very real. Radical Islamist group, Boko Haram, has recently come to prominence and seems to be operating with impunity in some areas. Following a mass prison breakout by its members in 2010, which saw the release of over 700 prisoners from Bauchi jail, in the north of the country, Boko Haram progressed to a campaign of bombings. Within hours of Goodluck Jonathan being sworn in as president, two explosions hit major shopping markets killing fifteen and injuring fifty-five. Two weeks later, Boko Haram instigated Nigeria's first suicide attack, hitting the Abuja police headquarters, followed by another attack a couple of months later on the United Nations building less than fifty miles from our training centre, before turning their savagery on to the nation's Christian churches.

With the president being a Christian, the risk of a hit is at an all-time high. But it isn't just Boko Haram that poses a threat. With ethnic division rife in the country, violent riots following the elections have already seen hundreds dead and the anger continues to simmer. It seems anyone from a Boko Haram suicide bomber to a mob to a lone-wolf type gunman could strike at the president and his aides, which means his bodyguards – the guys I am training – will need to be as good as it gets and to stay alert, big time.

We start off with the vehicle basics: walking to and from car drills; moving in and out of vehicles, and the transition to casualty evacuation, before moving to the more fun stuff: shooting out of cars. Fortunately, they all seemed super keen, including, surprisingly, Olu and Obe, my two sleeping beauties. We cover absolutely everything, to try to forge a team that actually can perform when the rubber meets the road. I show them how to take defensive measures when under attack and how to tackle the threat. We go through anti-ambush drills and the importance of planning the route, working through all potential scenarios and 'what-ifs'. Plus staying on alert in crowded places where they need to up their 'third-party awareness' – their ability to sense who poses the greatest threat. I then get them into executing two-car drills, where they learn the importance of positioning one vehicle to support the other, and vice versa.

That done, it's on to one of my all-time favourites: hand-to-hand fighting. I intend to take them through a series of un-armed combat sessions in the gymnasium, which I plan to get intensely physical. But like my other experiences of life in West-Africa, nothing is ever quite as straightforward as you might expect. Lesson one in unarmed combat: you need to know exactly what you're doing. Get it wrong and you'll get the crap beaten out of you. As a part of any physical combat demonstration, whether it's self-defence or hand-to-hand fighting, you need someone willing to play the assailant. It's usually a given that it's a *demonstration*, and so you're pulling your punches and just going through the motions.

But as I quickly realise, there is no demonstrating or play-acting with this group.

During my first session, I want to give an example of how to tackle an assailant one-on-one. I ask one of the lads, Adaebo, to grab me by the neck. No sooner have I finished my sentence than I find myself with a large hand and a crushing grip around my windpipe squeezing me for all his worth. My instincts kick in and I pull him in close, before knocking him off his balance, and putting him on the ground.

'We're demonstrating, Ade, my boy, not doing it for real,' I wheeze.

With a big grin on his face he nods, but I have an inkling that from now on there will be no more demonstrating – everything's going to be for real. I try again, reminding him it's only a *demonstration*.

'We're pretending, okay, Ade?' He gives me the same big grin.

This time, I decide I'll be the assailant but as I go to throw a pulled punch, he lands one back. Suddenly, he's firing on all cylinders and keen as mustard to physically fight me for real. Every time I try to demonstrate a move, he won't let me. Instead, Ade goes for the full-on punch-up. I like the warrior spirit, but as training goes . . . it's hopeless. Eventually, I have to put him in a proper headlock, just to restrain his more boisterous instincts.

I try a few demonstrations with some of the others, but by this time I've rolled around on the floor a good few times, and there's a few bloodied noses – none of which are mine. I will just have to accept that unlike in Western culture, where you can demonstrate hand-to-hand combat without needing too many hospital visits, in West Africa *every* fight is for real. If you're trying to demonstrate to a Nigerian and you ask him to hold your elbow and bend it like this, he'll grab your elbow and wrench it until it breaks. And that's just how it is.

Before long, things have begun to get seriously physical. We're fighting for real now, with real blows and the blood is flying everywhere. In the heat of the action everyone is just going for it, but I guess they are at least learning the key moves. As long as everyone gets out of this alive, we're all good.

Over the course of these very physical punch-ups – no point calling it 'unarmed combat training', because these are close to being full-on boxing matches – we begin to get to know the guys, and discover they're top-notch. Crazy as hell and seriously barking mad, but great company all the same. They invite us out with them into Abuja, suggesting we should hit 'downtown'. Now, I've been downtown in a lot of wild cities around the world, but downtown in Nigeria truly takes the cream and the biscuit.

Nigeria really is a tale of two countries. On the one hand, it's the poverty capital of the world; 60% of Nigerians live in absolute poverty, around a hundred million people surviving on less than one US dollar per day. On the other Nigeria has the highest number of black billionaires anywhere in the world, as I was soon to find out. For those with money, there's simply no limit to what you can spend it on and the crazier the better.

On our first visit downtown, we're taken to a series of hotels-cum-nightclubs to hit the beers. They're basically no different from your typical clubs back in Britain, but it's the clientele that sets them worlds apart. Sleeping in the gutter outside are the poorest of the poor, while arriving in a convoy of brand-new Humvees and Range Rovers are the nouveau-rich, waiting to splash their cash around.

There's a lot of money in Nigeria, most of it from oil. Nigeria is the world's sixth-largest producer. But the country's billionaires seem to have derived their fortunes from a whole host of fields, including telecommunications, diamonds and energy. Wherever we went, there seemed to be insane amounts of money sloshing around. It was like they'd plucked it off a money tree or printed off a stack of cash from the presses the night before. When a Nigerian wants to have a good time, very often the more excess the better, and he or she wants to be damn sure the whole world and its dog sees the cash being splashed.

On this occassion, I'm standing at the bar with the rest of the lads, and as I glance around there are people necking bottle after bottle after bottle of champagne. Apparently, Nigerians drink as much champagne as the French. As I watch the barmen prepare the drinks, endless trays of them being escorted around the room, each full of glasses of champagne topped off with a sparkler.

It's a big thing to put a sparkler in your champagne out here, if for no other reason than to announce to your neighbours that it's you who is mega-loaded and flashing the cash. It isn't long before the female 'escorts' teeter across the floor in our direction. In some weird kind of role reversal, the guys we're training almost become like our bodyguards now, expertly dispatching the less-desirable women back into the night, double quick.

In recent weeks, the Hilton Hotel – the one where we're billeted – held a special prize-draw with the winner receiving a brand-new Porsche. Somehow, they managed to manoeuvre the vehicle into the lobby where it sat all sleek and gleaming. A young Nigerian businessman staying at the hotel took one look at the car and decided there was no way was he going to wait for the prize draw, and face the possibility of not winning. Instead, he declared he'd buy the car outright. With barely a quibble the hotel agreed and the guy handed over the cash, but there was one – truly bizarre – condition. He wanted to leave the vehicle exactly where it was, smack bang in the middle of the Hilton for everyone to see, until he returned from a business trip abroad.

Nobody even batted an eyelid. The Abuja Hilton lobby had just become that man's very own personal car-parking space . . . and that was just how it was.

One night in Abuja we're taken on a tour to see some of the locals, who all seem to be having open house parties. One of the homes we go to seems to have a bottle of whisky embedded into the wall. I have to do a double-take before I realise it's all for real. While me and the lads are guessing how they got the bottle in there in the first place, we should have guessed it wasn't going to stay there for long.

This great big fat Nigerian guy appears, dressed in a shiny bright-blue suit and with his pockets stuffed full of cash. He proudly announces that he wants to buy the bottle of whisky, before pulling out a wodge of cash out and demanding to pay for it then and there. When the surprised owners tell him they'll have to arrange to have it specially removed, he dismisses them with a wave of his hand.

'No need,' he reassures them.

He promptly disappears, returning ten minutes later with some lunatic hefting a pneumatic drill.

As I watch in fascination, he takes the pneumatic drill to the wall and proceeds to drill the bottle of whisky out of it, plaster and brickwork flying in all directions. Classic. You could not make this kind of stuff up. After witnessing this, I realise that I have well and truly jetted into an alternative universe.

Back at the camp, we move onto the next stage of training. As part of their Presidential Guard duties, our trainees are not always going to be travelling by road, as a lot of time will be spent escorting dignitaries by helicopter or plane. We suggest they bring some of their air assets down to the camp, so we can put together an airplane/helicopter programme for them, and show them how to operate in and out of aircraft, including learning some perimeter security drills and the vital task of vetting and searching of all aircrew before commencing any journey.

A key part of my elite forces training was in such aircraft security drills, and I really want to share with them some of the essentials. They need to know this stuff, but it becomes clear the budget won't cover this part of the course. After watching Mr Pneumatic Drill's efforts on the wall of whisky, I'm sure if we really pushed they could find the money, but I'm in no place to say that. Instead, I try to impress upon them what a wasted opportunity this is. An air attack by Boko Haram could easily happen and they needed to be prepared. But we still can't force the issue.

We're nearing the end of the course by now – a course that will be sadly lacking in any air-security measures – and we put the presidential bodyguard trainees through their paces one last time. Despite my reservations about the few, I feel Nigeria's leaders are in pretty good hands. Oddly, we've never got to meet Goodluck Jonathan or any of his inner circle, but with the course at an end, the only task that remains is the settlement of our invoice.

If I thought Nigeria was a little crazy beforehand, I am in for an even bigger surprise when it comes to getting paid.

A day or so before we leave, one of the Interior Ministry officials arrives with a briefcase. By now Rich has flown in from the UK and like me he is expecting to see a cheque or similar, in return for all our hard work. But as the minister flicks open the catches and raises the lid, we're greeted by a big block of what appears to be US dollars; a couple of hundred thousand in clearly brand-new notes. We're told that we're receiving payment for the entire course in cash, and that we'll need to be careful at the airport because it is highly likely we'll get it taken off us.

I look at Rich and he looks at me and we try to decide what we're feeling. On the one hand, this is more money than we've ever seen, at least in raw cash, but the thought of it getting taken off us is stomach-churning. After we've shaken hands and taken possession of the case full of cash, the official leaves. Rich and I take a closer look at the great big block of cash; it's made up of consecutively numbered one-hundred-dollar bills.

My mind is racing. Where on earth did they get these blocks of cash? The whole thing is insane. I mean, you can't just ask the Nigerian Interior Minister – *Erm, is that entirely legitimate, sir? Don't you think you might manage a bank transfer?* It doesn't work like that in Nigeria. You don't ask questions; you can't ask questions. All you can do is you take the money, say thank you very much, put it in your pocket and sod off out of there.

But now we have a much bigger problem: how are we going to get it through the airport? We decide to split the cash up into bundles of ten thousand, and distribute it between the four of us, so that if one of us gets caught they hopefully wouldn't scarf up the entire stash. At one point we're wondering whether we should be strapping the cash around our bodies. It's then that I think of a cunning plan.

As one final exercise for the president's bodyguards in-waiting, we assign a very special diplomatic task: *escorting us to the airport and onto the plane, and without any delays or tomfoolery from any of the airport staff*.

'Right lads, this is your final task,' I tell them, explaining exactly what I have in mind. 'This is it: endex. This is where you put all of your training into practise. Show us you can do it. We expect nothing but the best from you – show us what you can do.'

Eager to impress, we get a first-class service from the guys: they not only get us to the airport, but channel us all the way through the gold-plated VIP channel, and all without any of us getting searched or having to answer any awkward questions. No quibbles; no nasty moments; no worrying scans – just a full pass for everyone.

Not long after we return to the UK, we learn that – tragically – our worst fears have come to pass. The president's men have had their first air fatality, and it's a serious one. Several government officials, including the former national security advisoer, General Andrew Owoye Azazi – a man who had long posed a massive thorn in Boko Haram's side – and the Kaduna state governor, Patrick Yakowa, were both killed, along with the pilots and some of the bodyguards who we had trained. They had apparently attended a ceremony and were on their way back in a navy helicopter, along with two of our team and the aircrew.

Five minutes into the flight, the helicopter exploded, before coming down in a ball of fire, killing all on board. It later transpired that a Boko Haram suicide bomber was onboard, posing as a member of the aircrew. If only they'd taken us up on our offer of an air-security programme, then every supposed crewmember would have been searched and the killer would never have been allowed to board in the first place.

Such a tragedy should never have been allowed to happen. I was saddened on learning the news. I'd warmed hugely to the guys we were training.

RIP lads.

CHAPTER FIFTEEN

HOBBY-GUARDING

In between the mad, the bad and the ugly of my private security work, I've dabbled on the celebrity circuit, bodyguarding the stars, or as I like to call it 'hobby-guarding'. The truth is that most of the time you're just a fashionable accessory. You're rarely there because there's a real and pressing need, although I have had to make a few timely interventions. One thing is for sure, I have never had any qualms about walking off the job if somebody was a complete idiot.

Life's far too short to be dealing with celebrities who are so self-obsessed they won't listen to good, sound security advice.

One of my first famous clients was the British MC and rapper, Dizzee Rascal, whose real name is Dylan Kwabena Mills. Dizzee was a great guy. I had to rescue him twice, actually, and both incidents were really quite funny. One weekend he'd booked an appearance at a local shopping centre, in Essex. It was crammed full of 12-year-old girls screaming their heads off. Dizzee was shaking himself in front of the crowd like he does, and some of the girls managed to get hold of his t-shirt.

They were tugging it this way and that and pulling it so tight that I could see the veins in Dizzee's neck bulging out. It was unbelievable that the T-shirt was still in one piece, which just goes to show that occasionally you can still get the odd quality garment in this day and age. My main concern was whether these hysterical teenage kids were going to strangle poor Dizzee. I always carry a small j-knife – a foldable survival knife – with me at these gigs, and I literally had to jump onto the stage and cut Dizzee's t-shirt off him.

The remains were thrown into the crowd, with all the girls screaming and fighting for them, while I got Dizzee restored to the stage, so he could continue his repertoire shirtless. It was priceless, really, and we both had a real good laugh about it afterwards.

The next gig with him was Glastonbury. Despite the T-Shirt shredding incident, Dizzee always wanted to be out amongst the crowd, and he was desperate to go and mingle with everyone in Glastonbury fields. I told him what seemed patently obvious to me: 'Dizzee, mate, you can't just go and walk around the crowds like everybody else – you'll get eaten alive!'

He was adamant that he wanted to go press the flesh, just to get a 'feel' for things on the ground and with the people. A part of me understood why.

'Here's what we'll do,' I said. 'We'll put a big woolly jumper over our heads and act like we're pissed, and we'll stroll through the crowds wherever you want to go, and no one will really notice us.'

Dizzee seemed fine with that. So, we got hold of this great big baggy jumper, and we somehow managed to pull it right over both our heads. The pair of us staggered about underneath it, walking through the crowds as if we were completely off our faces, moving unnoticed and unremarked right in the midst of all these hordes of festival-goers.

But all of a sudden, some lunatic just ran up to us and pulled the jumper off Dizzee and me. It came completely out of the blue, and I have no idea if the guy suspected who the figure beneath the jumper really was, or if he'd just got lucky.

Either way, Dizzee got recognized instantly. I realise he's going to get trampled on and seriously molested. This is potentially trodden-to-death stuff. I figure there is nothing else for it, but for me to pick him up, stick him over my shoulder and run like hell through the crowds, to get him back into the relative safety of the VIP area.

With hands grasping at us from all sides, that is exactly what I proceed to do. I manage to get him back there with relatively few, if any, rips to his present wardrobe. It was a job well done, and we both collapsed into a breathless heap once we're inside the VIP box, laughing fit to bust.

I travelled round with Dizzee on his tour bus, and found him totally chilled and a good laugh. We were driving to a gig one day and Dizzee was giving it all 'bare' this and 'bare' that, which is slang for 'a lot of'. So, 'There's bare people in that crowd,' would actually mean it was jam-packed.

I turned around and remarked: 'Yeah, Dizzee, I've got bare trainers.' That would translate to – I've got a wardrobe jammed full of the things.

Dizzee looked at me a bit weird: 'Yeah? Like how many pairs have you got?'

'No, Dizzee, I've got bear trainers. They're furry with ears on them.' I do actually have a pair of silly trainers designed to look like grizzly bears.

Dizzee stared at me with this raised eyebrow, as if to say 'you bleedin' idiot'. I think he got my sense of humour, which is a little off-beat and leftfield. Well, sort of.

A while later I got a new celeb client – Mika, the Lebanese-born singer-songwriter, whose real name is Michael Holbrook Penn-iman Jr. Mika's management approached me to bodyguard him during an upcoming tour of the Lebanon. Mika was born in that country's capital, Beirut, during Lebanon's long-running civil war. Frequent shelling would force the family to seek refuge in the basement of the garage in their apartment, before the family decided enough was enough, and emigrated to Europe, eventually settling in Britain.

Mika planned to return to the Lebanon to give a concert, as part of the Baalbek International Festival, a world-acclaimed music, dance and theatre festival held in the city of Baalbek's ancient Roman acropolis. I pitched up for the job, and there were meant to be two of us acting as his bodyguards, but Mika immediately sacked the other guy. 'No, no, I don't need two,' he insisted. In fact, he didn't really even want to have the one of us. It was only when those close to him persuaded him that he really did have to have at least one bodyguard, that he very begrudgingly kept me.

At first, Mika didn't want me to do anything for him and was really stand-offish. He was scheduled to appear at one of Baalbek's most-striking locations, an amphitheatre called the Courtyard of the Two Temples, situated between Baalbek's Temple of Jupiter and the Temple of Bacchus. It turned out to be an awesome venue, with these colossal columns over 20 metres tall that act as a backdrop to the stage and audience. But one thing struck me immediately – the nearest members of the audience were standing close to the stage at chest level, while those in rows behind rose up so they overlooked the stage.

Normally, performers are raised up on a stage above the audience, as that provides a physical barrier and an element of safety, as well as enabling the show to be seen by the crowd. With this kind of set-up, it left the artiste vulnerable. Mika didn't really want me anywhere near him on stage, but I was determined to do my job properly, and that meant that I would need to lurk just off stage, in case of trouble.

Half-way through the performance the inevitable happened. Seats had been arranged all around the amphitheatre, each with a square white cushion. Some idiot decided to be the first to lob a cushion at Mika. Due to its shape it flew like a Frisbee and pursued a perfect, lazy arc through the air, the stage lights catching it's fall nicely, as it plumped onto the stage. That was the big come-on. Everyone started to hurl a cushion or two. It wasn't exactly life-threatening, but after a while the entire crowd had joined in and were pelting Mika with a hail of cushions. The concert had turned into a massive cushion fight, with the stage literally covered in them. I figured it was kind of appropriate, considering the temple that formed Mika's backdrop was dedicated to the Roman god of drunken revelry and drama.

Mika began to throw a few in response, but that just egged the crowd on to unleash even more. I saw him glance about for help. His eyes came to rest upon the body-guard who he hadn't really wanted there at all – me. I could tell the pillow-hurling had really thrown and upset him. I made my way onto the stage and made it clear I'd stand by him for the rest of the show, as his protector. It got him through the remainder of the act, and after that he was like my best buddy ever. At one stage I was busy wading through the tide of cushions and hurling a good few back.

Mika never went anywhere else without me while we were in the Lebanon. Even if he was just going out for a meal with friends, he'd turn to me and say: 'Oh, er, Phil d'you mind . . .' Baalbek had been a complete game changer, and all down to a few cushions. I was glad we made the tour work. Mika returned to Lebanon several years later acting as goodwill ambassador with UNHCR (the United Nations High Commission for Refugees the UN Refugee Agency), for a cause close to my heart – the victims of the war in Syria. You couldn't have made a film like *Big Phil's War* (see Chapter Eighteen) and have seen and heard what I had, and not empathise massively with all those millions of Syrians who had been driven out of their homes by ISIS.

Mika spent time with the refugees and would go on to make a series of videos for UNHCR, showcasing their cause. It reinforced in my mind something I'd long believed: that people such as Mika could use their profile to support the kind of charitable causes that lay close to their hearts. For a long time, I'd felt like I wanted to give something back, and especially to young people who faced the same kind of horrendous life challenges that I had as a kid. I made a mental note then – when the time seemed right, I'd start to put some water back into the well.

I'd dragged myself up by my fingernails – from the kids' homes into the British Army, and from there to the pinnacle of the military elite, after which I'd lived it large on the private military circuit. Over two decades or more behind a gun I'd soldiered in Iraq, Afghanistan, Syria and across war-torn Africa – so in just about any hotspot in the world where there was trouble in the offing and guys like me were in demand. You could have said I was flying high, especially considering where and what I came from.

Trouble was, I was living something of a lie. This was the calm before the storm. And no matter what I did, or how deep I tried to bury the memories, the storm clouds were gathering, dark and angry and resentful and guilt-ridden and screaming-mad. Drink. Violence. The death-wish. I'd tried it all. I'd tried every means to bury my demons deep.

Unbeknown to me, I was about to crash and burn big time.

CHAPTER SIXTEEN

GOING DOWN

It was 2012 and I'd been a decade out of the British Army – ten wild years of living the high-life, of crazed adventures and mixing it on the private military circuit. But one evening I went out on the lash in my hometown, Southampton, and the birds truly did come home to roost. On that night, for whatever reason, it was my time to hit the wall.

I am a product of the system. Let me repeat that, with emphasis: *I am a product of the system.* For years, the system forced me into a place where I didn't believe I was worth anything and certainly felt that I had no right to speak out. I'd been told ad nauseam that I was a worthless piece of scum and to accept my lot in life. When you're a product of the system, it's so damn hard to bust out of that; to break the mould.

I'd been out drinking long into the night. As I'd sunk the pints of lager, the demons – the ghosts of the childhood abuse and the shame of the long years of silence thereafter – had come tearing out of the dark pit of my subconscious, as if it was unleashing all the dogs of hell. Cerberus – the hound of Hades – hasn't got anything on what I was being mauled by that night, deep down inside. I'd gone out with my partner Wendy aiming to get seriously pissed and either to forget, or to find someone – anyone – with whom to have a scrap and unleash some of the pent up aggression and rage.

I'd failed to find a suitable victim – I say that with no pride; with real shame – so I came back and snapped inside the walls of the family home. *Unforgiveable.* I smashed the windows, punched holes in the walls, tore apart the wardrobe in our bedroom with my bare hands. This was Southampton, and on the estate where I lived I was known to the local coppers: I was the troublesome, unhinged, former who-dares-wins type who believed he was untouchable. They came to the house mob-handed: two vans full of guys in all the right kind of gear.

The first policeman to make it to the upper floor got it big time from me – verbally at least. Of course, I was screaming out for help – but it was too late for any of that by then, for that wasn't how the police saw it at all. While they were thundering up the stairs they'd seen all my military plaques and photos; Commandos; Paras; Northern Ireland; who dares wins . . . The coppers piled in, every man jack of them wanting to make a name for themselves, and I went down under a whole rugby team.

Voices were screaming at me, as I was dragged downstairs in my underpants. Wendy was watching it all from the landing, her eyes saucer-wide, her face a mask of horror and pain.

'Get back in the fucking room!' I roared. I did not want her to see me like this. I knew what was coming.

Out in the garden the coppers leathered me – I guess in an effort to restrain me. Fists to the stomach; I was doubled up. Vomiting out a skin-full of beer. A skin-full of self-hatred and pain; of worthlessness. My mental health was so bad at that time I even told myself – *this is what you fucking deserve. This is all the system ever doles out to the likes of you. This is what you get: abuse and pain. Any cry for help – this is what you get. So shut the hell up, don't breathe a word and take it. Take it all.*

My last image was of Wendy, watching me get dragged away, bloodied and raging, by the coppers.

I was blue-lighted to the holding cells, but not for long. I'd barely got there when they had to blue-light me to the nearest hospital, due to this burning pain I was suffering in my chest. Maybe it was from where I'd had twelve burly policemen restraining me. Who knows? By the time I got back to the cells, they'd apparently decided what they were going to charge me with: *attempted murder*. Apparently, while I'd been wrecking my own home, smashing out some of the windows and screaming blue murder, someone had complained, and I'd told him to keep quiet or he'd be next.

That apparently justified the 'attempted murder' charge.

I asked to speak to the duty solicitor, and when she heard what had happened she advised me that on no account should I say a word to the police.

'Do not breathe a word,' she told me. 'Not a word. To ALL of their questions you simply answer 'no comment.' Got it?'

'Go it,' I confirmed.

That was exactly what I proceeded to do. After first being read my rights, the arresting police officers fired all these questions at me, some of which were utterly bizarre. To each and every one I answered 'no comment.'

On Monday morning I had to appear in court, for the initial hearing. I was mortified to see Perry, my nineteen-year-old son, in the gallery, along with one of his university mates. Perry was studying psychology, and he was forging the kind of path in life I might have followed, had the doors not all been slammed in my face. I was so proud of him doing so. But here he was, seeing his dad in the dock. I didn't even get to speak to him. I was marched in, read the charges, told I was remanded in custody, and marched out again. I could barely look him in the eye, I felt that guilty.

I was sent to Winchester prison, on remand. I sat in my cell, contemplating all that had happened over the last forty-eight hours. How in god's name had my life had come to this? Of course, this wasn't my first time on the wrong side of the law. I'd spent more than my fair share of time in the clink, while in the military and beforehand. But that was different.

Now, I was forty-five years old with kids and a partner; with responsibilities. I'd told myself I was done with those days – with getting myself locked up. But far from it. Here I was again. And this time, I wasn't just being charged with being drunk and disorderly or criminal damage – bad enough, but all excusable as high-spirited japes after a little too much beer. This time I was charged with attempted murder against someone in our street, with a dash of attempted GBH if that didn't stick.

That first night in the cell, I found myself sharing it with a young lad of nineteen years old. He was bawling his eyes out. Like me he'd had a drunken domestic with his girlfriend. Unlike me, he was a teenager and a delivery driver, just starting out on life's journey. By contrast, I was a long-lived military veteran with grey hair and a whole world of experience behind me at the hard end of operations. He had a right to be there, almost, and bags of time to turn his life around. I most certainly did not.

And in truth I did not feel a great deal better that he did. As I sat there contemplating what I'd just done, I was as low as I could get. I could get under a snake's belly with a top hat on, I was so downcast. When I tried to sleep, I found I was sobbing on the thin, narrow prison cot. I rolled away from that young lad; I did not want him to see me and to know.

During those first few days I did my best to help him out. I made a chess board and a set of players, so we could kill time by having bouts in the cell. Eventually, he disappeared down to B Wing, which was where all the drugs-dependent types went. I, by contrast, went to D Wing, where all the violent guys were sent. Those first few days were utterly horrendous, as I craned my neck trying to see out of the narrow window, imagining that I was not locked up in Winchester prison, but outside in the real world, breathing deep and free. I hate being locked up. I'd had more than enough of it as a kid in care. Yet this was no kids' home and there was no absconding from this place.

Not a small number of the inmates had heard who I was. Many of the guards had read my book, *Born Fearless*, which I'd published a year or so earlier, and which had hit the Sunday Times bestseller list. 'Not dead yet. Not kidnapped, tortured or killed . . .' read the cover blurb. 'Meet Big Phil Campion. To his fellow operators, he's a private military contractor. To you or me he's a mercenary, a soldier of fortune, a gun for hire selling violence to the highest bidder. But to Big Phil it's all just another chapter of a life spent fighting in the shadows . . .'

You get the idea of the rollercoaster story that my first book had related. But locked up on D Wing, having written such a book was like having a target pinned to your back, and especially as the cover has a mugshot of my good self emblazoned across it.

'Fucking what?' the prison guards sneered. 'Mr Born-fuck-ing-Fearless? D'you think you're gonna escape from here, big man?'

Loads of times I had that kind of thing levelled at me. I just had to shut the hell up and walk on by.

In D Wing they put me in this cell with a little Chinese guy who'd been arrested working in a hash-growing house (on the outside, a bog-standard residential address; on the inside, all the rooms decked out with tinfoil and lights and irrigation systems, so as to grow massive bushes of marijuana). I guessed he had most likely been trafficked to the UK by the Chinese Triads or similar. There were eight other of his countrymen on the wing, all arrested in the same sting and arraigned on the same charges: growing weed.

He showed me his paperwork, telling me he'd only got six months and that he was looking forward to getting the hell out of there sometime soon. Not a chance. When I checked his documents he actually had *six years*. I gave him the hard truth; there was no way to sugar-coat bad news like that. On hearing it he broke down in tears. When he shared the news with his eight fellows, they were all gripped with a similar sense of dark, tearful despair. Understandably so.

As I contemplated where I'd ended up, I told myself: *This is it. This is as bad as it gets. This is make or break.* I felt pretty damn certain nothing much would happen at my coming trial. I'd get off with some minor conviction or another. But that wasn't the point. The point was – how low did I have to get before . . . things changed. Before I changed. I made up my mind there and then: when I came out, things would be different. It was time to fess-up to some of my worst problems and to my past, and to turn my life around. Pretty much my last chance. And I figured I'd use my time inside to try to better myself, at least as best I could.

The prison offered lots of educational courses. Teachers came in to impart their knowledge to those who were locked up behind bars. Those doing time who were so in inclined learned, studied, got NVQs, GCSE, A-levels, even degrees. I wasn't going to be there long enough to become Professor Phil or Doctor Phil. But hell, I could cram-up on maths and try to get an NVQ, at the very least. I'd left school with no academic qualifications to my name. Literally none.

I knew how to wield a gun – just about any weapon ever made; I knew how to plant explosives – I could blow up just about anything (demolitions had been my specialism in the military); I knew how to protect important people and the super-rich, as a close-protection guy; I knew how to rescue those held hostage, how to kick down doors and make the bad people very dead and keep the good people alive; but that was about it. Like many ex-soldiers, I had very few Civvie-Street-friendly qualities.

I started to haunt the prison library. For the six weeks I had before me being locked up on-remand, I buried my head in books. The other big bonus about the library was that no one in there seemed to know who I was, or much care. But one day, on a whim, I blew that wide open. The librarian and I got on passably well, especially considering that she always seemed to wear the same bright-orange cardigan, and had a shock of untidy, spiky red hair, plus just the hint of a moustache, which I couldn't help staring at whenever I went to ask for a book. But this day, I decided to ask for something special, lest I forget who I was. Time inside tends to do that to you . . .

'Erm, any chance you've got a copy of a book called *Born Fearless*?' I ventured.

'Author?' she queried, glancing up from her screen.

It was on the tip of my tongue to say: *me*. But I could just imagine the kind of response that would get.

'Phil Campion. Or Big Phil Campion, as it says on the cover.'

She checked her computer and pointed me towards a stack of shelves. I went over, found the title and pulled it down. A hardcover. Well thumbed. My mugshot on the cover, eyes staring into camera, firm gaze; arms crossed. Shemag – chequered Arab-style headscarf – slung around my neck. *'Big Phil Campion . . . From Kids' Home . . . To Pirate Hunter. My Life as a Shadow Warrior.'* Yeah, well, if only all the readers could see me now. My life as a shadow warrior . . . which ends up with me in Winchester nick on remand for attempted murder, and cramming in the prison library to try to get a mathematics NVQ. I was deep in the shadows alright.

In an effort to try to shake off such dark thoughts, I grabbed the pen that the librarian put out on each desk each morning, and scribbled my signature on the inside page, under 'Big Phil Campion.' I could remember doing so countless times before, when we'd launched the book, and mostly at the request of those who'd purchased a copy and wanted the thing signed by someone they looked up to. Someone like me . . . How low the mighty were fallen.

I was pulled out of my memories – of a better time, a better place, a better me – by a cry from main desk. 'Hey! Don't write in the books! Please.' It was the librarian and she'd spotted me doing what she presumed was defacing one of the works of literature in her charge.

I wandered over with the book in hand and placed it on the counter, face down. 'It's alright. I don't need to read it,' I told her. 'I was there. Cover-to-cover, I was there.'

She shook her head, uncomprehendingly. 'Sorry?'

'Another life . . . I wrote the bastard thing.'

She just stared at me like I'd lost it. I guessed she must get quite a lot of that in here. I turned it over and glanced at the cover. 'Like I said.'

She stared at it for an instant, before realising what she was looking at. Her eyes darted up to my face and back again, just to be certain.

'Like I said, I don't need to read it. I lived it. I just signed it for you.'

She didn't say another word.

CHAPTER SEVENTEEN

THE CARAVAN KING

When it came to the trial, the entire thing was utterly laughable – unbelievably so. Having tried to stick charges of attempted murder on me, that first night in the cells, I stood in the dock facing a charge of attempted GBH. Even that fell apart within minutes of the hearing opening. Finally, the judge decided to leave the court, change out of his robes into a civilian suit, come back in again and announce that he was now 'acting as a magistrate.' In other word he'd downgraded the court from what the police wanted, so he could sentence me on the least serious charge: a public order offence – breach of the peace – which came with a £30 fixed-penalty fine. He told me I was free to go, while stressing what a complete and utter waste of everyone's time – the court's and the police's – it had been.

Amen to all that.

Still, I knew I had to be careful, once I got out of the nick. I was going to be on a 'tag' for six months – an electronic tracing mechanism. I wasn't allowed within fifty miles of Southampton, so I headed to London instead, which is actually where my birth mother hails from. A few years earlier I'd managed to make contact with my real parents, and I'd struck up a pretty good relationship with them, plus my uncles, aunts, brothers and cousins. Trouble was, none of my birth family were particularly well-off or with spare rooms in London in which I might camp for a bit, while I tried to get my life together after prison.

I also had a problem finding work. I'd fallen off the private military circuit for several months, and most people in the business knew why. A spell in custody wasn't the best of things to have on your CV, to put it mildly. In any case, I hungered for a new direction. I needed to turn over a new leaf, and to attain a new level of honesty with myself and with my past and re-establish my relationship with the wider world.

My cousin, Rick, was doing a building job in Sutton, south London, turning a five-bed house into sets of flats. They'd already gutted the building by the time he reached out a hand to help me. 'Phil, you can live in a caravan on-site,' he said. 'You do that, you'll have somewhere as a base in London and I'll pay you fifty quid a day as site security. You can pile rubbish into the skip during the day and do some building work, as part of the deal.'

It was all I had. Hell, it was a lifeline. I bit Rick's hand off. All I needed then was a caravan, but I had zero budget to buy one. I put a message out on Facebook. 'Pretty low right now. Desperate, in fact. Need a caravan. Any condition, as long as it keeps the rain out. A friend in need. Anything considered.'

I had a mate Tom, who, like me, was a former Para. He'd spent some time at RAF South Cerney, the Duke of Gloucester Barracks, and had left his caravan there. If I could retrieve it and get it mobile, I was welcome to it. For free. Not for the first time I reminded myself – that's what real mates are for. Pretty much everyone knew what had happened to me. The grapevine had been truly buzzing. But equally, they all knew – or at least a good number of them did – there but for the grace of God go I.

The caravan was a life line. I managed to scrape together enough cash to buy myself an ancient diesel Land Rover Freelander, and I headed for South Cerney in search of my new home. I reached the camp gates and told the guard my name and why I was there, getting myself a pass. Now, I had never laid eye on this caravan of Tom's – not even a photo. There was a big parking area where all those living on camp dumped their tow-alongs: boats, trailers, caravans. Each had a numbered lot, and Tom had told me his was on lot E203. As I drove up to the parking area, I was wondering what exactly I was going to find.

I spot a clutch of caravans, some of which look gleaming – brand-spanking-new. Now one of those would most definitely be alright. Trouble is, none of them carry the number E203. Then, out of the corner of my eye, I see it. It's green with mould, has moss all over the – uninflated – tyres, and the windows are so steamed up you'd think they had been painted white on the inside. I shudder to think what may be growing in there. Sure enough, as I draw closer, I see that this is the caravan parked on lot E203.

I sat there for a while just staring at it. Finally, I decided – in for a penny, in for a pound. Tom, bless his cotton socks, had posted me the key. I opened the thing up, only to get hit by a waft of unspeakable fumes. No way was I about to venture inside. I needed to get the thing mobile, get some air through it, and only then might I risk it. So I concentrated on pumping up the tyres – no punctures, thank God – greasing the axle, plus taking a butchers underneath it, to try to assess if Tom's caravan would survive getting dragged out of the weeds, let alone the tow to London.

It looked . . . driveable. Just. I did not have a number-plate to sling on the rear-side of the Freelander, so I grabbed a scrap of cardboard and a marker pen and scrawled out the number in big black lettering, before propping that in my back window. As I pulled off, I had visions of the Freelander keeping going, dragging the wheels and chassis with it, but leaving the body of Tom's caravan very much still in the weeds – like that classic scene from the movie Snatch, you know it. I return to the guard room and sign out. I can see the young lads staring at my battered 4 x 4 and Tom's caravan, thinking who is this sad hobo.

I set off towards Swindon. Suspecting that I wouldn't exactly get the red carpet rolled out wherever I tried to stop, I eventually pulled over on a garage forecourt that advertised a jet-wash car-cleaning service. I went to buy myself the requisite tokens for the car-wash machine. The guy behind the counter took one look at me, one look at the monstrosity parked up outside, and before I had so much as said a word he went: 'You can't leave that here, mate.'

If ever I had doubted the kind of prejudice automatically levelled at the gypsy community, I didn't anymore. 'I don't want to leave the bastard thing here,' I retorted. 'I want to wash it.'

The guy stared at me, one hand on his cell phone speed-dial and the other on the panic button below the counter. Eventually, I managed to convince him that I had not come to rob his store, eat his children and dump my caravan on his forecourt in the process. I paid for some tokens, spray-washed Tom's caravan, and it came up a little less of a green-grey shade of white. Before hitting London, I figured I needed a bolt-hole where I could give the thing the proper once-over and get it a little more shipshape.

So I headed for the Bisley shooting ranges, just to the southwest of London, where the 21 (SAS) Artists Rifles have their esteemed club house. I knew a lot of the guys there, including Steve, who is himself former SAS. I knew they'd give me a warm welcome – for all the obvious reasons – and no matter what kind of crap I had gotten myself into over the past few months or what kind of gruesome monstrosity I was towing behind the 4 x 4. Like I said, that's what real mates are for. Sure enough, I was able to park up the Mouldy Monstrosity to one side of the club house, and enjoy a good few pints of Guinness with the lads at the bar, in between tinkering with my new home.

Once that was done, the lads waved me off for London, with me praying the Mouldy Monstrosity would make it without falling apart on the way. Now I'm not exactly a small bloke and this caravan was a snug fit, let's put it that way. Still, once I got it parked up on-site with the jacks levelled up, sandwiched between the house's front window and the overflowing skip, this was it: home sweet home. Sutton has got some nice big houses, home to those who think they are . . . a bit special. I could see the neighbours to either side glaring at me, in a similar fashion as to how the garage attendant had, a few days earlier. I guess they didn't quite fancy the rest of the gypsy caravan flotilla turning up in my wake.

There was no way to cook in the caravan, but Rick took care of that: at eleven o'clock each morning, without fail he would march me down to the local greasy spoon, and order us both an Olympic breakfast. There was no loo in the caravan, or at least not anything remotely usable. Not a bother. In the mob that I hailed from the answer to that was simple and straightforward: from now on, I was on 'hard routine'. I'd defecate in plastic bags and urinate in a plastic bottles and dump it all down the nearest public convenience. There were no washing facilities, either. So, after a day on the building site I'd have to grab a bucket that had held bricks or cement of whatever, rinse it out under the one working tap, have a stand-up wash inside the shell of the building we were renovating and then, all-spruced-up, I'd hit the town – the caravan king.

The only trouble was, I had nothing smart to wear when I ventured forth to put the plan that I had hatched in prison into action. The answer to that had to lie in the local charity shops. During my lunch breaks I trawled those in the vicinity of the Sutton building site. In one I struck lucky. There was a beautiful Paul Smith suit, which seemed made to measure and it was all of £6.50. I snapped it up, and after dousing myself in a bucket of cold water and soap I got dressed in my glad rags and I was as ready as I was ever going to be.

I began frequenting my old London haunts: Le Beaujolais wine bar and The Ivy restaurant, both in Covent Garden – theatre district. My biggest hope lay in an old friend and contact of mine, seasoned reporter Toby Sculthorpe, who'd first forged a career in TV journalism with the BBC, but was now working at Sky News. Hailing from utterly different backgrounds and with utterly different life stories, Toby and I had bonded over the common sense of decency we'd detected in each other from the get-go – death before dishonour.

Take just one example, Toby was one of the few people from my previous life who'd deigned to visit me in prison. Regardless of how low I had fallen – bear in mind, my book, *Born Fearless*, was only a year old, and I was still supposed to be riding high on the wave of being a *Sunday Times* bestselling author, not languishing in the nick on charges of attempted murder – Toby stuck by me. Many did not. Those weeks locked up sorted the hangers-on and the good-time-friends, from those who really cared. Toby was one of the latter. In his book, it was exactly when your mates were at their lowest – when they were mired deep in the shit – that they needed you most.

In prison, I'd lost four stone in as many weeks, the food was so appalling. Toby became my life line: he brought me twenty Mars Bars at a time. On the first occasion, I decided to scoff the lot, saving one for Mao, as I'd nicknamed my diminutive Chinese cell mate. By the time I was back in the cell I had necked most of the bars, and barely had I handed Mao his when I felt the first rumblings in a stomach no longer accustomed to such an avalanche of rich food. Sensing the imminent evil revenge of the Mars Bar, I made a lunge for the throne – the toilet bucket, with which each cell equipped.

I proceeded to spend the next hour on it, obliterating any vestige of breathability or freshness that our cell might have had before-hand. Poor Mao was left to choke and cry on his cot, and needless to say his lone Mars Bar had been discarded – he had more than lost his appetite, as he turned green with the toxic smog that had invaded the cell we shared. But that was then, locked up in a stinking cell in Winchester nick with only Mao for company. This was now, in Le Beaujolais, a beautiful and historic wine bar discreetly tucked away on a side street, and frequented by a high-living crowd – a place where many a business deal had been plotted and schemed.

Toby had just landed a job at Sky as head of long-form news programming – basically, his role was to make forty-five-minute documentary TV programmes as spin-offs from the main news stories that Sky covered. I explained to Toby the plan that I had hit upon in prison – the Phil Campion survival and give-something-back plan. Surely, I explained, a guy like me, with a background in the care system who'd then made it into the military elite and had soldiered the world over – surely, I had a positive message to communicate to the public at large. I also had the gift of the gab. Undeniably so. I was never at a loss for words, and no matter the educational level or social standing of whoever I might be with.

Plus I had things that I wanted to say. My message was simple, but vital. I believed I could inspire youngsters to become what they want to be, and no matter where they had come from. No one should become a product of the system, as I had. No one should be told what they should be; have limits placed upon them; be taught to know their place. Even with my own kids I'd seen teachers tell them things like – you know, when you grow up you could be a van driver, for example; a delivery man. I felt like yelling – no! You could be *driven*. You can be whatever you want to do.

As a product of the system, I had carried that negative attitude as a burden for life; so now, my mission had to be to fight against it. And I knew full well how the military, despite all its shortcomings – and there are many still – could offer troubled youngsters from deprived backgrounds a route out of all of that, and a brighter future. Play your cards right, and you could get a proper education within the military; you could earn a degree even, and the military would sponsor you to do so. The sky was the limit, basically, no matter who you were or where you were from – and regardless of whether you were a product of the system.

I explained all that to Toby: these were then things I wanted to say. I just needed a medium. Could TV – could Sky – offer it? It wasn't that simple, Toby explained. We needed a compelling hook. A unique selling point. A reason why I, and only I, should be given that sort of platform.

'If we can find something you can do and no one else can, you've got an in,' Toby explained.

In other words, we stood a chance of getting me in front of the camera if we could find something unique I could add to the kind of programming he was producing. But try as we might, and over many a bottle of red at Le Beaujolais, we couldn't come up with anything. My cousin Rick had helped me when I needed it most, with the labouring job, but I couldn't do that for the rest of my days. I'd told Rick I was thankful, but I'd made it clear – 'I won't be here forever, mate . . .' I needed to come good on that promise; on the vows I'd made in prison.

Finally, after several weeks of living the life of the Caravan King, I turned to Toby, in exasperation one evening, and declared: 'Look, mate, I can see myself having to go back to Syria to do PMC work, if this goes on much more. I can't live in a caravan on a building site as a glorified rubbish-collector forever.'

Toby fixed me with a look: 'That's it! What a great idea. That's exactly what we'll do. We'll make a documentary about you going to Syria. To the frontline. To face off against ISIS. We'll start a series on foreign fighters – you're the perfect frontman to take the viewer into all those frontline situations.'

Well, I was a perfect product of the system – I knew that much. Products of the system didn't tend to make it onto mainstream TV, at least not in the kind of positive, revelatory way that Toby was suggesting. More often, it was as a suspect on *Crimewatch*. As a product of the system I was a nothing and all I deserved was nothing – that had been drilled into me ad nauseam. Only I could change that – this was me pulling myself up by the bootstraps. I'd had my come-to-Jesus moment in prison: you make your own life when you leave, you transform yourself and you become the message, or you're dead.

Toby was offering me the route into all of that. I had to grab it with both hands.

The first time I'd met Toby he'd said something to me I'd never forgotten. 'The media's a dog-eat-dog world. The bigger bastard you are, the further you will go.' Then he'd given me this very direct, piercing look and added: 'So, you are going to struggle, as you are a good bloke.'

At the same time, Toby could see I had my own way of thinking; my maverick leftfield streak; my independent self-starter mindset. He knew I would take myself into the dark side and get back to the light again. That was partly why he'd kept visiting me, all through the weeks in prison. He was never going to give up on me. He believed I needed just the one chance; the one break.

So, at Le Beaujolais, Toby and I plotted. We drew up a plan.

This was going to be all about a plain-speaking former elite forces soldier taking the viewer right to the frontline, right to the heart of these kind of conflicts, and relating whatever I found there through my eyes – through the gaze of a man who had spent so many years behind the gun, unleashing hell on the bad guys (or at least whoever the politicians in charge at the time had told us were the bad guys). In all the spin-off media – the background newspaper coverage, the breakfast TV shows, the radio interviews – I could slip in the underlying message: this is where I came from, and this is what I'm doing now. No matter who you are or what your background, believe in yourself: the sky is the limit.

Plan set, all Toby and I needed was a catchy title for the concept, something that did exactly what it said on the tin; something that would really grab the public's attention. After a few more glasses of wine, we hit upon it: we would call the film – *Big Phil's War.*

Of course, I was never going to follow in the likes of TV adventurer and former SAS man Bear Gryll's footsteps, but few people know war zones like I do, or feel so at home in them. Instinctively, I felt as if I should be taking the public to the frontline of battle, and offering them up close and personal experiences, ones they would rarely if ever experience with traditional journalists. What Sky really wanted was the sort of exposé that their regular journalists would find it hard, if not impossible, to secure.

Big Phil's War in Syria was just the ticket.

CHAPTER EIGHTEEN

BIG PHIL'S WAR

The invasion of Iraq and Syria by Islamic State, often known as ISIS or ISIL, had started in earnest in 2014. Early that year ISIS had launched an offensive to drive the Iraqi government out of key cities such as Fallujah and Mosul. Meanwhile, in Syria, ISIS took advantage of the discontent with the Bashir government, which escalated into civil war. By the summer of 2014, the world knew well the horrific brutality that ISIS had visited on the populations of both countries, through the media reports of mass killings, beheadings, rape and other horrific war crimes

Toby and I plus a small team at Sky started looking at our options for filming both in Syria and Iraq, and how we could make a truly revelatory film about the brave men and women taking the fight to Islamic State. We started off exploring exactly who were the foreign fighters engaging in a war thousands of miles away from home, risking their lives for a cause that you could argue wasn't theirs, although the battle against ISIS is a global one, of course. Surely, via their stories we had a perfect route into the conflict for any Western viewer.

We found dozens of websites and pages on social media plat-forms like Facebook, actively recruiting foreign fighters, and networking and raising funds for them. While the YPG (Kurdish People's Protection Unit) was the biggest recruiter, the most prominent pages were from the so-called 'Lions of Rojava', a group of Westerners fighting alongside various YPG units against ISIS ('Rojava' means 'the West' in the Kurdish language).

Most of the fighters I contacted were willing to talk to me and some even tried to recruit me: my military background was my calling card. Others were simply bragging that they were going to Syria to do this and that, but my bullshit detector was on overload. With those who were genuine, I wanted to find out who these people were, what kind of backgrounds they hailed from, what drove them to set off to fight ISIS, and whether they really knew what they were getting themselves into?

Once I told them I was making a documentary for Sky, several invited me to come film with them. The first two guys we interviewed were just out-and-out desperados. In fact, I ended up trying to talk them out of going to fight at all. I told them the truth: 'This is "man-town" we're talking about here. This isn't like a game of *airsoft*, or *Call of Duty*. This is for real and death is forever.' They hadn't seemed to understand quite what they were taking on, or quite how terminal it might prove.

We then found this interesting group which calls itself 'No Surrender', and is an outlaw bikers club based in Holland. Three of their members had travelled out to fight alongside Kurdish forces already, so they had credibility and prior form. We contacted them and they agreed to talk, so I travelled to Holland to meet them and scope it out. But unfortunately, just before we were about to go and film with them, one of their veteran volunteer fighters, Nomad Ron, died in a motorbike accident.

Regardless, the No Surrender guys encouraged us to film Nomad Ron's funeral. When we turned up at the venue, the Nomad himself was lying in his coffin on a table and all the members were drinking to him. It was somewhat bizarre. Afterwards, they invited us to the No Surrender clubhouse, complete with leather-backed chairs each inscribed with their logo. Although we did some filming with them, we were obviously there to explore Nomad and his mates' motivation to fight in Syria, but with Nomad gone, the others didn't really seem to want to engage and so we hit a dead end.

The next stop was Sweden, where we were scheduled to meet some American fighters, but it soon transpired that they were the worst desperados yet. None of them had any clear or credible idea what they were going to do or why. The only statement they seemed capable of making was: 'We want to kill Muslims'. When I asked the obvious – 'Why? What have they done to you?' – they did not have a clue. 'We don't care. We just want to kill Muslims.' I questioned one of them about how much he really understood about what was going on in Syria. His response: 'These Islamic people just need to be killed.'

What an idiot.

We left Sweden and Holland feeling as though we might as well pull the plug on the entire project. We were disappointed at what we'd filmed and felt uninspired by those claiming to have been on the front lines of the war in Syria, claims which in some cases I didn't even believe. We'd gone out seeking to discover some revelatory truths about what drove people to such extremes of action, which could easily cause them to die. We didn't feel as if we'd got anywhere near those kind of answers or met the individuals who were seriously committed to fighting ISIS, let alone reached a real understanding as to their motivation.

That's when I said to Toby: 'Why don't we just go over there and start filming what I make of the war? Sky can send as many reporters over there as they like but few of them know battlefields like I do. They'll have less of an idea what to look for and they've got little chance of gaining the kind of access that I can.'

It was going back to basics – to our original idea. And some-times – very often – the first idea is actually the best one. That decided, a few days later we set off for Kurdistan.

Once on the ground, the pace picked up. We were suddenly meeting fixers and mixers and all kinds of people, everyone prom-ising us the earth. I offered to do a spot of weapons training with some of the would-be fighters, in exchange for some footage. In no time at all we were able to meet these guys in Kurdistan who were all volunteer members of the YPG – the Kurdish People's Protection Unit.

'Right, come on down to the border, and we'll show you what's really going on,' they promised. We thought – *great, this is what we're after.*

We reached the Syrian border and ended up at a camp having a million cups of tea, as you do, meeting this commander and that commander, including some guy who hailed from Yorkshire and had a Yorkshire twang on top of his Kurdistan accent. After twenty years living in England, he'd decided to return and fight on the frontline for his people and for the cause.

This was more like it. This felt real.

As he and I were chatting, all of a sudden there was a right old commotion outside. Two pick-up trucks had come screeching up the road and skidded to a halt in a cloud of dust. Everywhere figures were whispering urgently and talking in hushed tones. Apparently, there was an attack happening on the border and we were told we needed to come down and film it right away.

My response was: 'Yes! Now perhaps we can get some action.'

I grabbed my body armour, stuck my helmet on and jumped onto one of the pick-up trucks. The cameraman leapt in beside me, Toby jumped into the truck behind, and moments later we roared off down this dirt track to what was supposedly the front-line. When we got there, there were hordes of blokes in combat fatigues lying on this earthen bank and they were all shooting in the one direction – towards Syria. I crawled up the bank to where the nearest figure was. He was yelling and screaming aggressively, and shooting long blasts with his AK47, giving it all the high-octane action stuff.

For a moment I glanced at him, and along the line of fighters acting similarly, before I realised that something just didn't add up: there was no one shooting back. I risked a peek over the top of the bank, and sure enough there was nothing coming our way: not a single round of incoming fire. It seemed as if we'd just been given the 'all-guns-blazing' show that they provide for every other news crew that turns up seeking a story. Unfortunately for them, I'd seen too many real battles to not know a fake one when I saw it.

I practically sat up at this stage, with my head and shoulders showing above the earthen bank. One by one the 'fighters' turned to me and stared. Eventually, I remarked to their leader: 'There's no enemy, is there? Where are the enemy? Where's ISIS? There's no one there'

Thinking on his feet, the guy came up with a crafty-sounding excuse: 'Oh, you know, they must have run away.'

'Really? Well they must've all run away at exactly the same moment and without shooting at you lot. There's no one there, is there?'

They finally realized that they'd been rumbled. Everyone looked a little shame-faced, to put it mildly, knowing the cat was well and truly out of the bag. I am sure they probably had had the odd tussle with ISIS at one point or another, but the battle had long moved on.

As we made our way back to the pick-ups, an air strike went in several miles away, but it had got absolutely nothing to do with them or their gun-fight show. We headed back feeling more than a little despondent. We'd come all this way hoping we'd get right to the heart of the story, and ended up with some guys giving it all the gung-ho Rambo effect.

Despite this, I decided it was time to give them a little bit of specialist training. I figured if they got a sense of who I was and my background, they might cut the crap and take us to where the real action – and the real story – was at.

I picked up an AK47 and went to test-fire it, but after one shot there was a stoppage. It was jammed up solid and I had to hit it on a rock to free-up the firing mechanism. It had a plastic handle and parts made from three different types of wood, and had clearly been cobbled together from several different weapons. But that wasn't the main reason it had jammed. It had a stoppage because it hadn't been cleaned of all the dirt and grit that finds its way into this kind of weapon in these kind of conditions.

It was probably just as well these guys weren't engaged in a real battle against ISIS, with this sort of weaponry, suffering from this kind of maltreatment. Unlike so many of the groups fighting them, ISIS have the luxury of modern US weaponry, which was given to the Iraqi Army initially and subsequently lost to ISIS. Meanwhile, the opposition mostly have to make do with battle-worn and obsolete weaponry, or stuff that's been cannibalised, plus a collection of volunteers who aren't always the best drilled. After all, weapons-maintenance is day one, lesson one kind of stuff.

As I delivered a stint of basic training for them, I was still wondering how we could get access to the real story. One of the foreign volunteers confirmed that there was a major battle going on in Al-Hasakah, across the border in Syria. I talked to one of the commanders and explained that was where we need to be. We spoke to the fixers, who promised they could get us to Al-Hasakah, no problem. Of course, the risks were legion, as we'd be entering into territory that was controlled by Syria's President Assad, which meant there was a fair chance that someone could betray us to the Syrian authorities. Worse, we could be kidnapped and sold to ISIS and be next in line for a beheading in an orange jumpsuit live on the internet. But those sort of risks come with the territory.

Even so, we're not taking any unnecessary chances. The last thing we need is to alert anyone to our presence in the country. Keeping a low profile and blending into the surroundings is the first rule in any such seriously hostile environment. I insist that we travel in local-looking cars with all the windows blacked out, so nobody can see there is a foreign news crew moving about. Inside, we'll all be dressed in shemags – Arab-style headscarves – so at a glance we can pass as locals. From the outside, it'll look like any other battered minibus crawling along the battle-torn streets, which is just how it needs to be.

Along with a fixer and a driver we move at the dead of night and manage to slip across the border into Syria. It's late and we have another good few hours' drive to reach Al Hasakah. The fixer suggests we should wait until morning and make the drive in daylight. I agree, but when he suggests we book into a local hotel to get some rest, I veto it. 'Not a chance.'

At a moment like this you have to ask yourself: although there appears to be no malice or bad intent, how well do I really know this fixer? In what way will he make more money, which after all is very likely his key motivation: by ferrying us from A to B, or by selling us to the bad guys? I tell the fixer we'll be staying at his house, which I know is not far away, as opposed to any hotel. That way, if he is planning to do the dirty on us, he'll be dragging his wife and children into the shit, which should act as a major deterrent.

In such a hostile environment, you want to secure as much firepower as possible. We're completely unarmed, but the fixer has a weapon. So when we reach his house, I insist I take his shotgun, for our own piece of mind. A single shotgun may not sound like much, but a top-notch pump-action Mossberg was actually one of my favourite weapons when serving in the military. This is because it can prove devastating at close quarters – and urban warfare is invariably at close quarters – as it blasts out a wide cone of death and destruction.

Our first night in Syria is spent sleeping on cushions on the floor of the fixer's house, with me using his shotgun as a pillow. We're imposing on his hospitality, but we've got no other choice.

Early the next morning we're back on the road, making our way down to Al Hasakah, where we meet some of the Kurdish commanders. One of them seems to get exactly why we're there and what we're after: he agrees to take us out to the frontline proper. That being said, Al Hasakah has what's called a 'fluid frontline', one that has changed hands often between the warring sides, which makes it an extremely dangerous place to be.

We're given a military escort – a gun truck – that leads the way. Our cameraman secures some great footage with the gun truck weaving through the cratered streets, but still there's no action. When we reach the frontline positions, there are echoes of what we saw earlier. The weapons leave a lot to be desired, the fighters have next to no ammunition and their drills aren't exactly top-notch. I end up giving them some on-the-spot training, but that isn't what we came for. Despite a few airstrikes, there is nothing serious happening here. *Where is the story?* There just seems to be no resistance from ISIS and very little fighting.

I'm frustrated at the lack of any real action, at failing to get to the heart of the matter, which is what I promised I'd deliver – and I can't hide it. Seeing my dissatisfaction, one of the Kurdish commanders tell us he'd like to take us to see the women. My curiosity is piqued: these must be the female Kurdish fighters of the YPJ's Women's Protection Units. I've heard a lot about these combatants, but I've rarely seen women on the frontline anywhere in the world – so I'm more than a little intrigued. I will end up being truly humbled to be amongst the Kurdish female fighters and to see them in action.

After all the disappointments, the Kurdish sisters will literally blow my mind.

CHAPTER NINETEEN

ZIRWAN'S STORY

Initially, the female fighters seem hesitant to speak with me. I guess they must be wondering what this 18-stone, shaven-headed former soldier is doing in their midst, especially with a camera crew dogging his every step. Curiously, I will finally manage to break the ice over some shared stories of tattoos, and tales of our different experiences on the frontline. Once they realise that I have been an elite forces soldier, and that I understand exactly what they've been through, both physically and emotionally, they open up completely.

Every single female fighter that I meet is here out of choice. Unlike some of the male fighters that I'd met earlier, these women aren't a bunch of conscripts (the Kurds do conscript into their forces fighting ISIS). The women are there because they believe in what they are fighting for one hundred per cent and are convinced that they are making a difference. They have all made huge sacrifices. Any number have lost family in the war, while others have been seriously injured, yet they've dedicated their entire lives to the cause. They may not have had the same training as a regular Western army, but their resolute strength and steely-eyed determination and passion shines through.

I'm blown away by their ballsy attitude. They are funny too, and they even get my off-beat sense of humour, which is a plus. I have nothing but respect for them. Zirwan, one of the youngest, is pretty and feisty, but also, like her fellow fighters, utterly focused on the cause. She believes men and women are equal in every way, and especially as fighters.

'We are all fighting for the same cause and fighting this war as one,' she told me. With a sparkle in her eyes, she added that she fancied that the women could even fight a little better than the men. I wasn't one to argue. Zirwan said she wanted peace for her people and for free peoples around the world. 'ISIS needs to leave. This is not a place for lawless terrorism; it is a place for humanity.' I told Zirwan I was right with her; I figured she was spot on.

We started to compare tattoos and she asked me about mine, as she'd seen a series of names etched on my skin. 'Those are the names of my children,' I explained. She showed me some family names on her arms, and joked that if ever ISIS got hold of her, at least they'd know where to send the body. Though Zirwan and the others had seen the brutality of war up close, and lost friends and loved ones, they were able to laugh about their predicament, just as any proper force of fighters is able to. They had that battlefield sense of humour that you only ever understand if you've been there and lived it.

I'm shown around their camp, the evidence of the savage fire-fights they've endured visible everywhere. Concrete walls are peppered with bullet holes. In one building, amongst the rubble and dirt, lie several dead bodies and dismembered body parts, which they've been keeping as battle trophies – including a foot hacked off at the ankle with the deceased's shoe still in place. It is seriously macabre, but who am I to judge? When faced with an enemy like ISIS, these women have decided to fight fire with fire. *Death before dishonour.*

They show me how they are operating, carrying out well-planned night-patrols, using gun trucks and snipers to detect any ISIS infiltrators who might have crept in under the cover of darkness. They take me to their prized rooftop position on top of a disused prison – memories of Winchester nick edging in from the shadows as we pass by the deserted cells – one that presents a panoramic view of the enemy's positions.

Their stories of extreme bravery and hardship touch me, especially when I speak to one young woman who arrives on crutches. Her left arm looks like it has been chopped half to pieces, her right leg is a prosthetic limb, and her left leg hangs largely useless. When I ask her what happened, I am told the most incredible, and utterly humbling, story. Quietly, calmly, she relates how she'd been trying to rescue some of her friends – fellow female combatants who'd been injured on the frontline – but in a fast-moving battle, by the time she reached them, she found herself trapped behind enemy lines.

As she got out of her vehicle she came under intense fire. Her right leg was shot to pieces, while her left was badly torn up. Regardless, she somehow managed to haul her friends into the vehicle. The two in the back were already dead, while a third, injured figure lay in the passenger seat, and a fourth sat across her. Though horrifically injured herself, she single-handedly got them out of there in that bullet-riddled vehicle, after which she was patched up after a fashion and had returned to the frontline . . . to continue the fight.

Amazing. What a woman. What guts. What courage. What sacrifice, for a cause worth fighting for. In short, the women of the YPJ are the most extraordinary fighting unit that I have ever come across, bar none.

Unexpectedly, out of the blue, this has become the heart of our story.

But I'm shocked that these women who are as poorly armed as the other fighters we've seen, are left to bear the brunt of so much frontline combat. Despite the odds against them, they are doing an unbelievable job. Zirwan, and some of the others, even did their best to draw some enemy fire while I was with them, just to show what they could do, but ISIS weren't playing. We never got a sniff of action from the enemy: ISIS feared the female fighters, knowing their die-hard dedication to freedom's cause.

Even so, Zirwan and her sisters had enabled us to secure some great interviews, plus footage of bombed-out buildings and the dead, but there was still no sign of any fighting – of the enemy. Instead of Big Phil's War, we now had Big Phil's Hearts and Minds, with bits and bobs of training thrown in. It was a shame, as I knew Zirwan and her sisters would have given their right arm to get a bite from ISIS and show us exactly what they were made of.

Having bid our farewells, we travel to Erbil, the capital of Iraqi Kurdistan, so we can pay a visit to a site that we've heard has just come under a vicious chemical attack, one engineered by ISIS. The minute we enter the area I can feel it in the air; there's no doubt that some kind of toxic substance has been used here. I can sense my skin starting to itch and my lungs tighten and burn. We head for the local hospital to meet the victims. They show us the terrible burns on their bodies – horrific red sores that look as though the skin has been eaten away. It's clear evidence of the use of such banned weapons and its horrifying. It's another emotive, shocking story for our film – riveting testimony to the evil incarnate of ISIS – but while I am seeing all the evidence of war, I'm not seeing *war itself*, which is what I promised.

It's time for Toby to fly back to the UK, to start to edit the material we've shot. But as he leaves, he reiterates that message – we're still lacking the very heart of the story we came here to try to capture. We need to get into the heart of the action; to the centre of where the real fight is. Part of me suspects that we have been fobbed off by all these senior Kurdish commanders; that they're deliberately *not* taking us to the real action. I have a suspicion as to why.

I figure they think that having a TV crew around their fighters might actually jeopardize their ability to wage war. Which makes me think that those of us on the Sky crew who are ex-forces need to be allowed to take our own course; to go one step beyond; to find our own way. Sky agree that we can make one further attempt, but this time I'll go in just with my cameraman, Dickie, an ex-Royal Marine who has bucketloads of experience, plus the one security guy, John, who is ex-SBS (the Special Boat Service, the sister unit to the SAS).

We've heard from the various foreign fighters that there is a place called Sinjar where some of the fiercest combat is presently underway. Situated in northern Iraq, Sinjar was one of the main areas inhabited by the Yazidis – a non-Muslim people living along Iraq's northern border with Syria. On the 3 August 2014, Sinjar – the Yazidi's foremost city – had fallen to Isis, who were intent on erasing the Yazidis from the face of the earth. Between 40,000 – 50,000 Yazidis had fled into the mountains.

The refugees were stranded there without food, water or shelter, relying upon whatever supplies could be airdropped by Western and Iraqi forces. Within a week, the Kurdistan Workers' Party (PKK), the People's Protection Units (YPG) and Kurdish Peshmerga forces had opened a corridor from their territory into the mountains, relieving and safeguarding around 30,000 Yazidis. But it was estimated that at least 7,000 Yazidis women had been taken as slaves, and 5000 – men, women and children – had been killed.

But whenever I mention Sinjar as a potential filming destination, I'm greeted by gasps and looks of horror on the faces of the Kurdish commanders. It's as if I've asked them to take us to the depths of hell itself. They don't want to even talk about it. Perhaps it's understandable, considering the atrocities that have taken place there. Either way, they agree to take us to meet some of the Yazidis themselves – men, women and children who were chased out of their homes, hunted remorselessly and are now in a nearby refugee camp.

Nothing prepares me for the stories that I'm about to hear and the pitiful sights that I will see. I meet women who were gang-raped and beaten by ISIS members; I hear the horrendous and heart-breaking story of one young woman who attempted to flee, but was caught, shot twice in the head and raped repeatedly. She survived, but was left severely brain-damaged. Her mother,

Arzan, struck me as being an utterly extraordinary and coura-geous woman. She explains how ISIS have taken all the women of her family bar her – including her daughter, her ten-year-old granddaughter and her auntie. She tells me how ISIS have done horrendous things to her ten-year-old granddaughter. For someone who was himself abused as a child, my very blood boils.

I'm utterly humbled by Arzan's dignity and her towering strength. How she has found the will to live, despite everything, is beyond me. At the same time, I'm sickened to the depths of my soul by such unspeakable actions, and such evil child abuse. I've seen and heard – and suffered – some horrific things in my own life, but this is perhaps the vilest I've ever learned of. At one stage Dickie decides to turn the camera on me, and interview me, to capture my emotions.

I find myself unable to continue speaking, because I am back in the realm of my own childhood, trapped in the abuse, and I am fighting back the tears.

I meet some of the kids in the refugee camp. Despite an interna-tional outcry at the fate of the Yazidis, little has been done to help them and many may be condemned to spending an entire lifetime as refugees. As we drive away, I find myself thinking about my own children. Again, I'm welling up at the thought of some of those amazingly-spirited kids in that camp, who have done absolutely nothing to deserve the terrible situation they find themselves in. It breaks my heart.

After the Yazidi experience, we go to meet Mazar, one of the highest-level commanders for the Peshmerga, the official military force of Iraqi Kurdistan. Over yet another cup of tea I tell him a little bit about myself, my background and why I'm making this documentary. I outline all that we've filmed to date and explain how we're missing the one thing that we really need: shots of those on the frontline, fighting the battle for real.

Mazar leans back in his chair and looks me up and down, a little doubtfully. 'But how are you elite forces? You are too fat! Much too fat to be an elite soldier.'

Admittedly, I have put on a bit of girth since the glory days and I have to admire Mazar's straight-talking attitude. But at the same time I can feel the hackles rise on the back of my neck. I'm genuinely put out that he thinks I'm trying to sell him a pack of lies. We've struck up something of a rapport, so I decide to give it to him straight.

'That was over ten years ago. Tell you what – if you doubt I am who I say I am, bring your hardest men here and I'll fight every single one of them, and then we'll see who's hard.'

Mazar eyes me in silence. I think he's waiting for me to crack up laughing and admit that what I've just said is all a big joke. It's not. Far from it. I may be eighteen stone, but I can still mix it with the best when I'm called upon.

Each year I organise – and I fight in – the Remembrance Rumble, in which British elite forces veterans box against their American counterparts. Last year I fought a former US Navy SEAL who was at least ten years my junior. Regardless, it was still myself who walked out of the ring with my head held high. I say this not to blow my own trumpet. We run the Remembrance Rumble to raise money for veteran's charities. I say it to illustrate that I was quite happy to go toe-to-toe with Mazar's meanest, if need be.

'Look, I came over here to show you lot fighting a war,' I add, 'and so far I've not seen anybody shooting a gun at anyone remotely like a genuine enemy. It doesn't look good for you lot, does it?'

He asks me why I want to see fighting so much – why it matters. I tell him that I need to show the conflict on Sky, so the British – and world – public will understand the ferocity and savagery of the people they're up against – ISIS – and the poor weaponry and kit with which they are forced to fight. At its simplest, the war against ISIS is a war of modern civilisation against barbarians. It is all of our fights. I want the word's public to see how we're failing to support those on the front line of that struggle.

I make a pledge to Mazar. If he gets me to the front line, when I return to the UK I'll go to the British Parliament and I will show the politicians just how it is for him and his men.

'I want to see if I can get troops on the ground, or at least proper equipment, to help you guys fight. At the very least I want to ensure the UK continues with the bombing campaign – the air strikes. I cannot do that if I have no evidence of your troops fighting the good fight. At the moment all I've got is bullshit: people playing at being soldiers far from the frontline.'

Mazar still seems doubtful. He argues that we could endanger his men, if we get in the way. 'If you're going to become a burden and a hindrance, it is best you stay away.'

I figure it's time to play hardball. 'Listen, Mazar, if it gets that bad we will down our cameras and pick up weapons and fight alongside you and your men. We'll join in the combat if we have to. That's the deal.'

All three of us are capable of doing just that and more. Alongside myself, John, the former SBS guy, has seen more action than Rock Hudson, and Dickie, the cameraman and former ex-Royal Marine, has soldiered in both Iraq and Afghanistan.

I leave Mazar to mull over what I've said. By morning it seems to have done the trick. It turns out that Mazar has looked me up on the internet – don't you just love the modern media world we live in – and realised that I am who I say I am. He agrees that if we sign a waiver – basically agreeing that we have ignored his warnings and are the authors of our own doom if things go wrong – he'll give us passage to Sinjar.

We sign on the dotted line and pretty much right away we set off, intent on finally witnessing what the hell is going on.

We leave Mazar's base in an armoured truck, in the company of a cadre of his fighters, our escort to Sinjar. For hours and hours we jolt along this never-ending dirt track, as the sun beats down. All being well, it will take us directly into Sinjar and onto the frontline. As time passes, I realise what a horrendous set-up we're getting ourselves into here. The Kurdish frontline positions are perched on this triangular-shaped hill rearing in the distance, and which looks almost like a three-sided pyramid. While it offers a fabulous vantage point, it leaves those positioned there completely exposed.

Mazar has warned us that ISIS will be able to see us, as we move into that position. If they realise exactly who we are – for them, we're ultra-high-value targets – they may be able to surround us, at which stage there will be no way out. At the time I thought he was just trying to put the frighteners on us, to dissuade us from going. Now, I realise he was just telling it like it is.

We pull up in the lea of a stretch of war-ravaged grassland, that acts as the no-man's-land between the two frontlines. I'm helmeted and have my flak jacket strapped onto my torso. In the circumstances I'm about as protected as I can be, yet I've never felt so exposed. I've only just stepped out of the truck when I hear the unmistakable sound of the first mortar round being launched by the bad guys. There's no time to do anything but dive for cover, and so we huddle by the rear flank of the truck.

There's a brief few seconds of a banshee-like wail, before the round slams into the ground less than 25 metres from where we are hunkered down, throwing up a whirlwind of rock, earth and shrapnel. It strikes me that this is some shit-hot shooting: ISIS must have their mortar zeroed in on this spot, just awaiting an opportunity to open fire. The adrenalin starts pumping and my heart's thumping like a jack-hammer. We wanted a fire fight and now we've finally found one.

Within seconds, another round slams into the ground on the far side of the truck, blasting jagged fragments into the steel sides of the vehicle. Momentarily, the air is thick with dust, blinding us to the chaos. I'm semi-deafened and reeling from the blast-wave, but one thing strikes home most powerfully: the ISIS gunners now have us 'bracketed'. Having dropped one round to one side of the truck and one to the other, by rights the third should be bang on target – and that will be the end of the truck and of us.

A third mortar goes up. It lands just yards from the rear of the vehicle. The ISIS gunners are working overtime to keep their hot and smoking mortar tube lobbing out the rounds. As the explosions keep edging closer, Dickie, the cameraman, John, the security guy, and myself are in the heart of this battle, which is good news for the material we're filming, but it may prove terminal for us. It feels like a case of be careful of what you wish for . . .

With no obvious cover other than the truck, it's human instinct to stay where we are, cowering like frightened rabbits. The problem is, if we stay put we're toast. The only other option is to make a run for it, but it's at least forty metres to the safety of the nearest cover – one of the Kurdish trenches. If a round hits when we break cover, they'll be picking our dismembered body parts off this hillside for a good while to come.

I'm suddenly reminded of the detached foot that I saw earlier, with Zirwan and her sisters. I really do not want to give ISIS the satisfaction of parading any of my dismembered body parts around, like some prize they've won at the fairground.

To the banshee howl of the mortar barrage is added another sound now: the crack and thump of light and heavy weapons exchanging fire. Bullets start pinging in all around us and ricocheting noisily off the armour of the truck. As muzzles spark all along the Kurdish front line, the terrain is lit up by this otherworldly deep-yellow glow. It's clearly now or never, if we're to make the dash for the cover of the nearest trench.

Dickie, the cameraman, is the first to move. I watch him jink and twist, as he dodges the spurts of incoming fire, camera in hand. I'm next. I tense my muscles, reminding myself of how difficult it actually is to hit a figure running at full speed – a lesson we learned time and time again in the military. I burst out of cover, sprinting up this shallow gully formed by an open, dusty track. The bullets are howling and snapping all around me, but somehow I manage to dive into the lea of a pile of sandbags without being hit.

I lie there, lungs gasping and thanking my lucky stars that I did not take a bullet. I roll over and beckon to John. He's the last of us to make a run for it, and with two having gone ahead of him he's taking the greatest risk of all. The bad guys will have seen the two of us execute the sprint of our lives and they will be waiting.

As John breaks cover I'm shitting bricks that he's going to get a mortar round rammed down his throat.

CHAPTER TWENTY

SINJAR

Fortunately, John's younger, and wiry and lithe compared to my mature muscled bulk – he flashes across the killing ground like lighting, lines of fire stitching up the dirt at his feet. He dives into cover not so far from Dickie and myself, and yells out that he's okay. I breathe a huge sigh of relief. I realise I've been holding my breath while John made the charge.

I grab a moment to take stock. Above is the rocky ridge that overlooks the ISIS stronghold, deep in the valley below. Dug in just below that are the main Peshmerga forces, readying themselves for yet another upsurge in the fighting, one prompted by our arrival.

We're taken to meet the overall commander, Brigadier General Muhamed Rashid, a big, wiry Kurdish guy in his late thirties. He explains that for the last forty-odd nights they've been fighting continuously. Every night without fail there's been a raging gun-battle. He warns that we need to stay close and within the area he specifies, because he expects the fighting to intensify. If ISIS get word of our arrival he figures they may experience combat intensity here the likes of which they haven't seen for an age.

John, Dickie and I work our way along the ridge, so we can meet the troops. They're all Kurds from northern Iraq. The youngest

is probably no more than eighteen; the oldest are already griz-
zled veterans by their mid-twenties. It's immediately obvious that
they've seen a lot of fighting. They're visibly tired, weary and
battle-worn, yet they're way more switched on than any of the
units we've met so far. They're actually actively seeking out the
enemy – scouting about, not just sitting tight.

The light begins to fade, the flares of tracer bursts cutting
across the darkening sky. The troops start to filter out into the
forward-most trenches, as they move into their fighting positions.
At this point there's still a part of me questioning whether they
might just be doing this for our benefit – another Ramob-esque
display for me and the camera. I decide to take a wander about,
just to get a handle on how genuine all this activity is.

But then the first serious burst of incoming fire erupts, and the
entire force manning the frontline does stand-to – just as business-
like as we would, in the British military. No one's bluffing here
and it looks as if things are about to get very serious indeed.
Everyone's facing towards the enemy situated down in the Sinjar
valley, weapons at the ready. It's there that the Yazidis have been
burned out, kidnapped, raped, and hunted from their homes and
murdered by ISIS, in their thousands.

As the source of the incoming fire creeps closer, increasing in
accuracy, I realise this means that the ISIS fighters are drawing
nearer, using the cover of darkness to do so. The guys in the
trenches to either side of me start whistling and yelling names.
I can't understand a word, but it's somehow hugely eerie and
spine-tingling.

I ask Mazar's man – the guy he's sent to accompany us – what exactly is happening. He tells me it's their nightly ritual of taunting the ISIS fighters.

'What are they calling them?' I ask.

'They call them whores and dogs and all sorts of other names to try to goad them into revealing themselves.'

As I'm crouched down behind the sandbags listening to this weird exchange of frontline insults, I'm aware that as the Peshmerga yell out one thing, ISIS respond by yelling something back. It's completely insane. The yelling and screaming between the two factions intensifies, before finally the whole place explodes into a full-on fire-fight – one massive, adrenaline-fueled all-out battle.

The ISIS gunners start to throw more and more mortars at us, and the air is filled with the intense howling of their trajectories. Each ends with a ground-shaking thud, as the round detonates, rock breaking apart as the mortar explodes, showering death and destruction all around. The night-dark air is thick – almost burning now – with tracer rounds, as an intense barrage of gun fire hammers in towards our positions. The frontline is under heavy attack and bit by bit the terrain to either side of us is being blown to pieces. It's carnage.

John, Dickie and I try to move, darting from position to position and staying low, but it's beginning to feel like we're surrounded. From where the armoured truck is parked up, we detect the sound of intense fighting, as the battle reaches some form of a crescendo, and so we make a move back towards that terrain.

We reach a 'pinch point' – a narrow neck of friendly territory, surrounded by hostiles – and there seem to be bullets coming in from almost every single direction, including behind us.

Predictably, they're zooming in on the armoured truck, which up until now had been our means of making an exit from here. We know we need to make it further up the track, so we can get under some proper cover, but every time we try to make a move there are bullets pinging around like swarms of angry bees.

You could say we're pinned down. We're also right on top of the Kurdish guys who are returning fire. Dickie is getting some great footage, literally filming over the fighters' shoulders as the muzzle flashes from ISIS fighters blast out from the opposite direction, right down the lens of his camera. The volley of fire is so intense, I can see the frontline positions silhouetted clearly in the flash of all the gunfire.

In the middle of this mayhem, all of a sudden I hear the familiar ring tone of someone's mobile phone going off. It's one of those surreal moments when you can just imagine how the conversation might go, or more likely the voicemail. 'Hi, you're reached Omer. Sorry I can't talk right now. I'm just in the middle of a raging gun battle and could well have my head blown off at any moment.'

But it's now that Dickie realises exactly whose phone it is that's ringing. It's his own. In the mad dash across here he's managed to drop it smack-bang in the middle of the track, where the crossfire seems at its most intense. Someone is trying to call him in the midst of the night during the most epic firefight. The ringtone is persistent and it isn't stopping. Dickie is furious, but only because it's ruining his footage. This is surreal: Vodaphone's ring-tone is not the sound-track anyone would expect to be hearing right now. I tell myself there is no chance of retrieving it or of stopping the call; anyone who steps one foot onto that track is signing their own death warrant.

I've barely had the thought, when, from the corner of my eye, I see John, our security guy, spring to his feet and hurl himself across the track, executing the most dramatic combat-roll I've ever seen. In one swift motion he dives, rolls, snatches the phone, rolls over again and dives straight into a ditch on the far side, where he proceeds to calmly switch the damn thing off. That move was beyond awesome and totally insane, but it literally saved the day in terms of the soundtrack on Dickie's footage

Eventually, the fighting slows and it goes quiet for a bit. We gather around the dented and battle-scarred armoured truck for a breather, when one of the Kurdish fighters decides he wants a word.

This guy, Mustafa, approaches me and asks: 'Can I do a selfie with you?' He's got the inevitable mobile phone clutched in one hand.

'Absolutely, mate,' I beam.

As I stand with Mustafa in the middle of this war-ravaged track, I give my best happy-snappy look as he prepares to shoot his selfie. But the big surprise is yet to come. In his eagerness to get his shot, Mustafa has forgotten to turn his camera's flash-function off. So, there's a big white flash of light, and in that instant the mug of yours truly – plus Mustafa – is lit up like a beacon for all to see, on both sides of the battlefield.

This is like the mother of all 'oh shit' moments. I hear the ISIS guns spark up again, just as he and I make a dive for cover. For what seems like an age we're pinned beneath this murderous barrage, purely because Mustafa wanted to grab a selfie.

The fighting continues like this for an age, before we finally get a proper lull. We take the opportunity to move back to the commander's bunker and the main fortifications. General Rashid has been here for months now, so he's well-seasoned and I want to get his take on the bigger-picture side of things. He tells me they don't have enough ammunition, the weapons are breaking-down daily, and they have to conserve, repair and make-do-and-mend with everything.

Compared to ISIS, they are horrifically badly equipped – ISIS having armed themselves with what the Iraqis left behind, after they capitulated in Mosul. ISIS have modern weapons and more ammunition than you could shake a stick at, most of which is made in the US. The Peshmerga, by contrast, have very little. They need to preserve their firepower, so they can sustain the nightly fire-fights, which tend to last for four or five hours. Tonight's, General Rashid explains, has been a little more extended and fraught, no doubt due to us being there.

Everything is in limited supply; even food and water is rationed. We've sensed as much already. When we had dinner with them that evening, it was very much just a scoop of boiled rice and a tiny little bit of sauce to go with it. Nothing was wasted, because they knew how easily they could be completely cut off down here.

We're in the middle of our chat in General Rashid's bunker, when we hear a massive, deafening explosion erupt from just the other side of the ridge. The tremors of the blast shake the entire hillside, and the intense pressure in my head from the blast makes me wonder if my ear drums have burst. We get word from the guys above that an ISIS suicide bomber has driven a vehicle into one of the nearby buildings. The explosion has been massive and the rising cloud of black smoke and dust engulfs the whole area, bringing visibility to zero.

Within seconds the fire fight begins all over again. I'm now just outside General Rashid's bunker, hunkered down behind a wall of sandbags. A thin slit lets the troops keep watch on the enemy. I decide to take a gander for myself. As I peer through the gap, there's an immediate swish, and a crack like that of a whip, as a bullet comes tearing through the slit. It's missed my head by a bare few millimetres. I've just very nearly had my head taken off by an ISIS sniper. General Rashid has seen the whole thing, including me whipping my head back in shock, and he seems to have found it really quite funny.

'Be careful, Mr Phil,' he chuckles, 'you need to make it back home to make this film. Have you got what you came for?'

'Yeah, more than we could hope for. It's been great.' I beam a smile back at him, although inside my stomach's gone all to jelly. That close a near-miss tends to do that to you.

'This is our world,' he tells me. 'This is what we do every day. Now, hopefully, you can share our story with the world.'

'That's exactly what I intend to do,' I say, shaking his hand.

Several times during the fire fight I have admired his cool, calm and collected approach to command, even in the midst of the heat of battle. General Rashid is a top man in my book.

I take a moment to reflect on the long night's events. These Kurdish forces have managed to hold ISIS off, but there is no doubt in my mind that if the bad guys had seen a way of storming our positions, they would have done so in a heartbeat. It's all to the troops' credit, considering the amount of heavy and persistent fire they've had coming their way.

For the next hour Dickie, John and I continue moving from position to position up and down the frontline. Dickie's getting amazing footage and I decide to take a wander round the various gun pits. While I'm unarmed and have to keep behind the guys, I'm able to help give them target indications, and direct fire, identify enemy positions whenever they've lost sight of the ISIS fighters.

Just as the sun begins to rise, turning the horizon a pale salmon pink, the fighting begins to die down. The past 24-hours have been extraordinary, and I'm in awe of these men. They are so different from any of the troops we've seen previously. They are conserving what little ammunition they have; they aren't trying to get rid of it in a spray-and-pray show for the cameras. They've been out here for so long and have seen so much fighting that they've attuned themselves to the nightly flux of ISIS operations. As for us, we finally have the footage we came for and enough to tell the story we set out to tell.

At first light we get back into the truck that shielded us from so much of the fighting last night and we execute the dash back up the hill. As we do so, I am amazed the vehicle has survived and is still usable. No sooner have I entertained the thought, than a mortar round comes howling in, smashing into the rough terrain just behind us. Our driver steps on the gas and we speed ahead leaving a cloud of sand in our wake.

When our film finally airs, both on Sky Atlantic and on Sky News, it attracts a whole lot of attention. I'm interviewed on

The Eamonn Holmes Show, and he asks me why Sky sent me out to Syria.

'Eamonn, when you watch a football match, who are the best pundits? It's Gary Lineker and Alan Shearer, people who actually know the game because they played it, so why should the battlefield be any different? My job in the military . . . was primarily to gain information, bring it back and report accurately what's going on. I don't bend the truth; I tell you the truth. If I tell a lie and say there are fewer people than what there are, there's a good chance that someone else going in and acting on my intelligence will die. There's no agenda with me – I just tell you the truth.'

When I look back at my time in the military, a battlefield is a battlefield. You understand when you're being shot at; you understand how things work. I trained for that environment my whole life. This is where I am comfortable; it's what I understand. Reporting from a frontline like Sinjar was all about gathering information, putting my experience into a package and bringing it back alive. The battlefield is a great leveller, perhaps the greatest there is; you either understand and get it, or you don't.

We were able to tell the story we had because the three of us – myself, Dickie and John – were able to go out and work alongside friendly forces. We weren't reporting on them, we were reporting with them. It's the hearts-and-minds concept all over again. Forging relationships with people and taking the time to do something with them and for them; forging a bond with somebody in a moment of crisis when they're fighting for their life. That's what gets you there; that's how hearts and minds works. The perception that you've actually taken the time to do something for them and with them is invaluable.

At the end of the day, the documentary we made rated better than just about anything that Sky News had put out on screen that year, and online it proved equally popular. Perhaps most importantly, I was told it contributed massively to the decision made on the 2 December 2015, when the House of Commons approved British airstrikes against ISIS in Syria.

The film had received a private screening in Parliament, and it had had the impact we'd all hoped it would. I'd been there, with Toby and the film crew. I'd presented the documentary to the distinguished committee and taken questions afterwards. I had kept my word to the Kurdish commander, Mazar, that I would present his case to the British Parliament in person.

But mostly, I'd let the film do the talking – and just look what it achieved.

CHAPTER TWENTY-ONE

PRODUCT OF THE SYSTEM

In truth, I hadn't achieved what I needed to on my life-journey. Baring my soul in front of the Birmingham audience had been a watershed moment, and it hit me just when I thought I'd really topped-out. I thought I'd laid my demons to rest, forged a new career path which afforded me the platform to speak up and be heard.

Mental illness is like that: it creeps up on you when you least expect it, blindsiding you when all your defences are down, and maybe because you don't believe you need them anymore. You're free of it all. You've made it through. Only, you haven't. There's one more hurdle. You'll never know until you jump the first one.

The event organisers had put me up in a hotel the night before, as it was a long drive from London, and so I'd be fresh for the speaking events the following day. I'd had a good night's sleep, no thoughts of my childhood plaguing my dreams; no nightmares of the abuse rearing their ugly heads. Not the slightest hint of what was coming; of the dam that was going to break.

During the long drive from London in the Range Rover I'd treated it like just another talk in the diary – on the speaker circuit – something that had followed on naturally from my book-writing and TV career. It was billed as another typical Big-Phil-makes-it good-pulling-himself-up-by-his-boot-straps inspirational kind of a story. That's what they'd signed me up for.

If the guy before me hadn't spoken up as he had, telling that story of one child's journey through hell and how crucial it was that others speak up to stop it happening; to bring an end to the abuse – if he hadn't stressed repeatedly how not enough people are willing to tell the grim truth, and especially amongst our age groups, it would never even have crossed my mind to diverge from my prepared script. As it was I sat there listening to him, like a rabbit caught in the headlights. As he spoke about the conspiracy of silence, I thought: *That's me.* I thought: *What are you? A man or a coward? You're doing people a huge disservice if you don't talk about it; that's betrayal. You need to stand up and get it out in the open; if you don't you're part of the problem. You're one of the conspirators.*

As I didn't know a soul in that room it was just that little bit easier for me, or so I kept telling myself. As the guy was winding up I just kept repeating in my head – *let them have it and see what they say.* Even so, as I got up to speak, the applause from the guy before me drifting away to silence across the auditorium, I felt like I was stumbling forward in some kind of a dream. You know that kind of out-of-body experience when you almost look down upon yourself, separate from who and where you are, like an observer; a voice whispering – *no, come on, he's not really going to do this, is he?*

That's exactly how that long walk to the stage felt for me.

Even as I reached the podium and took the microphone, I still wasn't decided. I was still at war with myself. Could this great big hulking tattooed shaven-headed former elite forces soldier really tell it like it is? Did he have the balls; the courage; the humility; the honesty? So like I said, this truly was my who-dares-wins moment. Nothing before or since has ever come close.

Once I'd finished speaking, I wanted to run – to get out of there as fast as my weak and wobbly legs would carry me. But of course, I was expected to stay – to take questions and to press the flesh; to meet and greet. In no time people were mobbing me, telling me how astoundingly brave it was of me to have opened up as I had. But of course, no one quite realised the earth-moving gravity of the situation that had unfolded spontaneously, unexpectedly, and had been a total shock to me. Forty-plus years of unimaginable torment had spilled out in front of a room packed full of strangers, none of whom I knew from Adam.

I was the guest speaker – the top of the bill. I'd been promoted as a product of the system, but also, crucially, as a success story. Proof that the system worked. Got results. This is how we can do this, was supposed to be the basic message. Look at Big Phil; look at how we succeeded with a guy like that, from such challenging beginnings, against all odds. I'd been billed as someone who would stand up and say how great the system was; that was not what they had got at all.

After I was finished, I was in shock, and I just wanted to flee; to get in the Range Rover and drive. Home. Away from my spontaneous confessional. Away to somewhere safe; a place where everyone didn't know my darkest, innermost secrets, ones that had twisted me and tortured me for all these years. Mired and trapped in a dark, shameful silence, at least I had been safe. Invulnerable.

But now these two hundred people knew, and maybe they might use it against me. Or maybe they'd resent me pricking their bubble; telling a story of how the system – their system – could be such a dark and spectacular failure for a kid like me. But as more and more people came up to me, the reaction proved hugely reassuring and uplifting.

'That was truly amazing. I wish I could hear that all over again.'

'More and more people need to do that, at your stage of life. So brave.'

'Wow. That was far better than anything I'd ever been expecting in my wildest dreams.'

In turn, I found myself telling people: 'You know, I wish I'd done it all a lot earlier. People used to warn me – if you say anything, you'll be the one in the shit. You're nothing. You're the scrote; the loser. It will never work. You open your gob, you'll get more shit on top of shit.'

I explained how I had carried the fear with me for my entire life, no matter where I went and no matter what I did, and not matter what I achieved. No matter how those around me viewed my achievements – soldiering in the military elite, writing the books, doing the TV shows – deep down I'd carried that fear with me every step of the way. If you speak out, if you tell the full unexpurgated truth, you're finished. Until that moment I'd spoken to no-one at all, not ever, not once. Not even to the woman I loved – my partner, Wendy.

It's still hard to explain how I felt right then. I felt like I'd gone back to the very beginning. I felt like I'd had a massive re-boot to the system. Been re-born almost. I felt about ten tonnes lighter;

like I was walking on clouds. But at the same time I felt shaken to the core, wobbly, hugely emotional and yes, almost fragile. Vulnerable, certainly.

There had been another pressure on me not to speak out, one that I figure predominates in the macho military culture in which I was forged. It's the fear that people will turn around and say: 'He's just trying to justify his time in prison and all the trouble he got into in the military.' There is always that threat, which was instilled in me since my earliest years, my very beginnings; keep your mouth shut. When I was a toddler getting beaten about by my adopted 'father' – punched in the nose and with blood splattered across my nice clean school shirt – my adoptive mother had kept urging me: 'Just tell them you fell over at home, Phil. Keep your mouth shut, Phil. For your own good. It's better that way.'

After that, it was the authorities in the kids' homes trying to keep me quiet, either because I'd witnessed them sexually abusing other kids, or because they'd tried it on with me; or succeeded with me, in Terry's case. After which it extended to so very many others in my life, including some of my commanding officers in the military. 'Keep quiet about it, lad. You don't want to stick your neck out. It'll only end badly for you.'

I was still surrounded by people who wanted to chat at that Birmingham venue, as first the guy who'd spoken before me, and then the lady who was hosting my visit, told me they had to leave. As for me, I'd just broached the most intimate taboo in my life – a paedophile got his penis out in front of me . . . I was feeling more than a little agitated, and I kept telling myself – *As soon as I get the chance I have got to get out of here.* Eventually, I too managed to slip away.

As soon as I was out of the door, I just kind of stopped on that pitch-dark street and felt myself hyperventilating. *What the hell have you done? What the hell have you just gone and said?* Over all those years I'd never breathed a word to anyone. Now, I'd blown the whole sordid tale in front of all those people – just thrown it out to an open forum. Were there reporters in the audience? Would it be in the newspapers the following day? I just didn't know.

I found myself walking back to the car, thinking what next? Where do I go from here? I did not regret it, but I was ripped apart with all these conflicting feelings. First, there was the flood of relief – *Finally, I've done it.* But then there was the feeling that I hoped to hell it'd been worth it and it helped someone; that I hadn't just done all of that for nothing. Finally, there was a rump of utter disbelief that I'd actually done it. I got back to the Range Rover as if I was in a dream. I eased myself behind the wheel, and this massive crushing wave washed over me – a tsunami of all the stuff I'd bottled up for all those years.

As I had done so many times before, I sat there thinking about all the bastards who had abused me – it welled up and boiled over. This was the kind of moment that normally led to a massive drinking binge, to scrapping and, most recently, to prison. But this time it was different. Normally, I'd find these moments catching me utterly unawares and they'd torture me. It would boil up and I'd force it back down again, but the collateral damage could be close to terminal. Inevitably, I'd head out for a pint or ten and get real nasty with people; drink and violence was the only way I knew to bury it all.

But this time it welled up and boiled over and spewed out the top of my head, and it was gone . . . The release, pure and simple, was amazing. If I can talk about this in front of two hundred strangers, I told myself, I need to call the one person who I love most and talk to her about it all; to show her that I have the guts and the honesty to do so.

I called Wendy, my partner and my future wife, and with the mobile hooked up to the car's speaker system I let it all come flooding out. I am not ashamed to say that I sat there on that darkened Birmingham street and I let the tears flood down my cheeks as I talked and she just . . . listened. I left it on speaker phone and as I just wanted out of that town, I started to drive. I needed to get away and to get my head around what I'd just done.

I talked to Wendy for most of the drive back to London – for hours on end. It was like a gradual awakening. I told her what was becoming clearer and clearer to me: if I've done this now, then I'm going to do this again, there will be no half measures anymore. I need to make a difference – there is no point otherwise. I want people to know about this – let's identify how these predatory paedophiles operate and how they influence and keep others quiet; the power play. Yes it does happen; let's expose it. And let's expose the mental health issues that flow from such trauma, and the conspiracy of silence surrounding it all.

Another thing struck me so powerfully. Had I realised earlier I could have spoken out earlier, and my life could have been so different. Had anyone encouraged me, I could have dealt with it and processed it and empowered myself and slain my demons many years ago. I would dearly love to have finished my career in the military elite and to have made it to regimental sergeant major (RSM). I never got the chance. Instead, I fell out of the military and fell into private military contracting, which was all I knew how to do.

Should that make me bitter? The lack of support, understanding, help? Maybe it should, but frankly life is too short. I don't have enough time on this planet for the people I love, let alone those that I don't – those who refused to reach out a helping hand. I need to concentrate on the stuff that benefits me and my family and those that I love. All these thoughts – all these words – passed between Wendy and me on that long drive to London. That was the watershed moment: between silence and speaking out; between being part of the cover-up, the conspiracy, and honesty. Between night and day.

Shortly after that long night's drive, I got on the phone to Bear Grylls, who I knew from our shared military pedigree – we both had strong links to the Royal Marines (I'd completed Army Commando training, after the Royal Hampshires and before becoming a Para, and Bear was an honorary colonel in the Royal Marines). With Bear's 21 SAS background – the territorial unit – needless to say we had plenty of friends in common.

I told Bear about my desire to speak out about mental health and to use my story to inspire a younger generation, especially those who might be tempted by a career in the military. I told Bear how I felt it would be irresponsible not to let my story go out as widely as possible, now I'd broken the silence. Mental health and PTSD and suicidal soldiers on the rebound from Iraq and Afghanistan – more and more were finding the strength to speak out, but more and more were likewise losing the will to live, mired deep in the darkness.

I knew this, from personal experience. Ever since I'd joined the Royal Hampshires, I'd taught myself to prepare for the possible deaths of some of those I was close to. I accepted death in combat. Wherever I came across it, I accepted it, no matter how close a mate I might just have lost. It's not easy, but you teach yourself to do it. Yet suicide is a whole different ballgame. Each one hits you so hard, as it's people you know so well losing their lives for . . . nothing; for often preventable reasons. What I find hard to accept is such unnecessary death; life is too precious to be wasted. So when I look back on all the suicides of those I knew well – some of my closest military buddies – those are the deaths that have really affected me.

Since I joined up countless people have killed themselves due to bottling up their issues. Suicide is a mental condition which is a massive problem within the veteran community, both in the UK and the USA. If people addressed their mental health properly and early enough, you could stamp a lot of it out, and speaking out is the absolute key. If veterans don't feel that it is acceptable for them to do that, they never ever will. By the time they make their final call for help, it will sadly prove too late – terminal. A cry from beyond the grave.

I explained to Bear that I hope people can look at a guy like me, and think – if he can break the silence, so can any of us. The trauma of combat and losing your closest mates is cumulative and so is the potential damage it does to your mental health – it's okay to say so, to speak out. To admit: *I have problems*. It's the silence that kills. Of course, I had all the childhood abuse grafted onto the cumulative stress of the battle trauma, so that very likely was a double whammy, mental health-wise.

Which begs the question, had I ever felt like ending it all? The honest answer of course is – *Yes I have*. Several times. Most recently, and the worst of all, was when I was locked up in Winchester prison. I was literally on the brink at times there. But whenever I've entertained those darkest of thoughts, I've told myself this is really a cry for help, and if you end it all you're beyond help, aren't you, so that isn't exactly going to work. As Winston Churchill famously said, and I expected I'm paraphrasing here: 'If you're going through hell, keep going.'

Each time I felt that urge to end it all, I managed to pull myself back from the brink. In a way being a product of the system gave me a peculiar kind of inner strength. I was unable to talk to anyone as a kid, as there was no one I could trust, so I taught myself to talk to myself. I do that still, to this day. Likewise, I talked myself out of my suicidal thoughts and those darkest of moments.

All those who may have suicidal thoughts or mental health issues need to know it's okay to speak out. They have to know they can go to someone and talk, without feelings of inadequacy, shame and the fear that the military, or their Civvy Street employers, will kick them out because they've shown that at heart they are what we all are, which is, quite simply, *human*. If we don't get this message heard loud and clear, traumatised soldiers will keep killing themselves, hurting their loves ones, and messing up the lives of their nearest and dearest. Drinking. Taking drugs. Turning to suicide as a last, desperate act.

It's the same old same old: 'Tommy this and tommy that . . .' The poet Rudyard Kipling wrote about it all those years ago; about not being able to talk about these kind of issues, for fear of the impact it would have on a veteran's social standing or his employment prospects. It was a massive issue back then in Kipling's day, over one hundred years ago, and it remains so today. As Bear said, we need to change that. We need to speak out. Strong, not silent. All together now – strong not silent.

Break the silence.

It's time.

CHAPTER TWENTY-TWO

REMEMBRANCE RUMBLE

I've always had a thing about boxing – well, fighting in general to be honest – but I've never really had the time to properly learn to box. As you get older, you start to reassess your fitness goals and I realised I needed something to motivate myself. Thanks to a very good friend of mine, Wayne Batten, who's a professional boxing coach, I was introduced to the Peacock Gym, which proved a true inspiration for me. It's an amazing place and has been one of London's best loved and respected community gyms for decades. It's turned out several champion boxers in its time – Frank Bruno and Lennox Lewis, to name but two.

I started regular training with Wayne, and after a while and I declared the obvious: 'I want to have a fight.' There didn't seem a lot of point training and training and training, if I wasn't ever to put myself to the test in the ring. The problem was Wayne struggled to find an opponent for me. Most of the boxers were either novices, and their response was: 'Well, I'm not fighting him, knowing his military pedigree.' Or they'd be professionals who had previously boxed in a hundred fights, and they'd just turn around and say: 'Happy to fight him, but there's no point, 'cause I'll beat him.'

I was having a drink one night with a friend of mine. We started talking about boxing and I mentioned how much I wanted to have a fight. He said: 'Well, I know a bloke who used to be in G Squadron – Rob Paxman. He's a big fellow. He'll probably fight you.'

We phoned him up right there and then and I said: 'Rob, do you fancy fighting me for charity?'

'No problem, love to,' said Rob, straight away.

Rob and I announced the fight on social media and I contacted a friend of mine, Graham Hampton, who was putting on a series of fights via an events company called White-Collar Boxing. These are bespoke events in which people with no prior boxing experience, working everyday nine-to-five jobs, get the chance to train and to fight at a top venue. I asked Graham if Rob and I could promote the fight through his events company.

Graham's response was legendary: 'Yeah, of course you can. You'll be top of the bill.'

Once word got out it went absolutely ballistic. It seemed everyone was talking about these two elite forces types having a tear-up (fight) for charity. We both chose our nominated causes. I decided to fight on behalf of Care After Combat, comedian Jim Davidson's charity, which provides assistance for the care of veterans and their families. Rob chose to fight for his own charity, Talking2Minds. Talking2Minds promotes itself as being 'founded by Rob Paxman (former 22 SAS), with an ethos of veterans helping veterans'. It mostly works with those suffering from post-traumatic stress disorder (PTSD), and other stress-related conditions.

In short, we were going to fight in aid of two fabulous causes.

Rob and I took it in deadly earnest. We went into full-on

intensive training, and at the same time we began this relentless, crazed online banter, just to really big the thing up and drive ticket sales. We took the piss out of each other non-stop. Rob took to calling me the 'Hampshire Hamster,' because my nickname in the boxing world was the 'Hampshire Hammer,' as I do have large hands and I did grow up in Hampshire. Rob was known as 'The Spartan' in special forces circles, so I took to calling him the 'Spar Shop'. For weeks on end we had this toing and froing slanging match on social media, but all in the very best of taste and one hundred per cent for the cause.

On the night of the fight, the banter had reached fever pitch. Just prior to entering the ring, Rob was still pulling ugly faces and grizzling. He'd chosen to turn up in a Spartan helmet, which was great theatre. Finally, we got in the ring and proceeded to batter seven bales of shit out of each other. It was a fabulous night and we'd raised a shed-load of money for the two charities, which was awesome.

After that, Graham, who'd run the event, posed the obvious question: 'Well, lads, where do we go from here? That was a great night, but can we do it again and can we make it better?'

'How about if I put a team of former SAS guys together,' I suggested, 'and then we get a team from America, made up of our opposite numbers, and we fight? How does that sound?'

The universal response from everyone was a great big: 'YES!'

I started making approaches and I managed to get the first few members of the Brit team on-board. Rob Paxman was well up for it, as were some former SAS and SBS buddies. Amongst the high-profile Brit veterans who stepped up to fight were Channel

Four's *SAS: Who Dares Wins* luminaries Colin Maclachlan and Mark 'Billy' Billingham. Next I contacted a friend of mine in the States, Brandon Webb, who was a former Navy SEAL. In a heart-beat he recruited six fighters from the US military elite, and our very first International Remembrance Rumble was announced.

We secured the backing of the *Sun* newspaper, and the endorse-ment of British heavyweight boxing champion, David Haye. David got right into the banter. He was quoted in the *Sun* giving the Yank team a right good verbal battering. 'This is a message to all those SAS boys going up against those sissies, the Navy SEALs,' Haye remarked, in a video message delivered from his boxing gym. 'You can do all their training in about two minutes. We know you guys are the real deal, so it's going to be no issue . . .'

The Rumble was held in a historic boxing venue, York Hall, Bethnal Green in the East End of London. No winners were declared on the night, but let's just say the British contingent – yours truly included – gave a very good account of ourselves. The *Sun* ran the blazing headline: 'Remembrance Rumble charity boxing match is a big hit . . . SAS soldiers fight US special forces in charity showdown.' The article went on to say how, 'The *Sun*-backed charity was the brainchild of "Big" Phil Campion, 47 . . . He battled ex-US Marine John Schneider . . . Phil said: "I'm ecstatic and humbled."'

We would go on to hold four further Remembrance Rumbles, it became one of the bigger events of the veteran charity's calendar. The Rumble is one of the things that I am most proud of in my life. If anyone had ever told me when I was in Lakeside Lodge kids' home – groper's paradise – or even at Kingham Hill – where they'd nicknamed me Council House Kevin – that I'd end up founding an international charity, with celebrity and press backing, raising thousands of pounds for veterans, I'd never have believed it. But with the Remembrance Rumble that is exactly what I'd achieved.

It's good to give back. Putting water back into the well. But still I wanted to go one step further.

Ever since my time in various children's homes, it had always been my ambition to be able to help other kids growing up in similar circumstances. I wanted to be able to share my experiences and my insight, so that the next generation could learn the right lessons, and hopefully have an easier start in life than I had, not to mention some better prospects.

It wasn't until a couple of years ago that I felt the time was right to do something to fulfil that ambition. By then I'd begun to build my public profile. I'd written four books and I'd appeared on national television in several programmes, and as a guest on channels like Sky News. I was building up a following on Twitter and Facebook and was beginning to get messages from young people asking for my advice. I felt I needed to take the plunge and find a youth organisation to champion.

The Scout Association obviously has Bear Grylls, who does a fantastic job, so there was little I could offer them. Besides, for a worldwide brand like the Scouts I really don't have the global name and recognition that someone like Bear has earned.

In the UK, I was well aware of the outstanding work being achieved by the British Army Cadet Force (ACF), one of the country's largest and oldest voluntary youth organizations. Because of the media coverage that I'd been gaining, I had been invited to make a couple of appearances at various branches of the ACF. I found that I loved it. The Army Cadet Force constitutes a 100,000-strong organization of 12 to 18-year-old recruits, plus adult volunteers. They were doing exactly what I'd always wanted to do, which was helping the next generation develop the confidence to overcome the challenges they faced in life, while inspiring them to go and achieve all that they could.

I contacted the office of Major General Duncan Capps, General Officer Commanding Regional Command of the British Army, to float the idea that I might act as some kind of ambassador for Army Cadet Force. I was surprised when they replied almost immediately, and with enormous enthusiasm. After a meeting with the ACF team in Aldershot, they decided to announce me as the champion for the Army Cadet Force, at FrimFest, in 2019. This was when the Cadet Training Centre at Frimley Park opened its gates to the public for the very first time. It was a fantastic day, and to be the official 'Champion' of so many young and ambitious people felt like a dream come true.

One of the things I was determined to ensure was that I was seen as someone to whom the cadets could truly relate. Being the ACF champion is very much a grassroots role, in which I hope that I can pass on the benefits of my experience to the young lads and lasses involved. I want to be close to what they're doing, so when they invite me to their summer camps as their ambassador, I'll be there painting my face along with the rest of them, rolling around in the dirt and marching up and down the square. I hope I'll be seen as very much as one of them, as well as being something of an inspiration.

In short, if you can come from the kind of – let's be frank about it – hellish upbringing that I had, and still make it to soldier with the best, and go on to greater things, well . . . anyone can. You don't have to be a victim of where or what you come from. My life is living proof of that. At age seventeen, after Terry-the-bastard's abuse, I was in a dark place and I had reached a crossroads. My life could have gone in one of two directions: into a life of crime, prison and worse, or into the British military.

I chose the latter course, thanks to the good advice of the one or two people who were around me at the time who genuinely had my best interests at heart and who saw something in me. I could so easily have gone the other way. If I had, I doubt very much if I would still be alive today. It's really all as simple as that.

My biggest ambition right now is to attract more adult volunteers to the ACF, because without them the movement can't function. I've spoken to numerous people about joining and recruited quite a number. I'd like to set up an academy where training can be offered, which I hope will attract more volunteers. To anyone who is ex-military, I'd like to end with an exhortation. If you're missing the green skin and fancy the chance to pass on some of your invaluable experiences to the younger generation, please get off your backside, get back in uniform and join us! The cadets will welcome you with open arms.

So, come on in, the water's lovely.

CHAPTER TWENTY-THREE

WHO DARES WINS

Unfortunately, the kind of bullying that I hoped I had escaped in the kids' homes and at times in the military, reared its ugly head again, in recent years.

When I'd published my first book, *Born Fearless*, I still had this cloud over my head. I still believed it was somehow unmanly to speak out – about either my mental health issues or the childhood abuse. I still believed all those who had told me that – (a) it would do no one any good – (b) it would do me more harm than good if I exposed my major issues in life – (c) no one cared or would do anything about it, anyway. But if you look at your life honestly the only person you can't lie to is yourself. If you write a book you can hold back whatever you like; you can airbrush out the ugly bits. But if you're going to be brutally honest, you have to let the entire lot be told, warts and all.

Back then, when writing *Born Fearless*, I didn't think it would benefit anyone. Now I do.

Following *Big Phil's War* – the Sky TV documentary – I started to do a lot of social media (podcasts, videos, tweets) about the kind of abuse and mental health issues I'd suffered. Let me tell you – the greatest response I ever get is concerning such issues. I cannot remember the number of times I've received a tweet or a Facebook post or an email from someone telling me how much that kind of honesty has helped them with their own state of mind, or in their own life struggles. Sadly, all too often, they are former – or even serving – soldiers.

But without that one chance encounter at that Birmingham conference on fostering, I doubt if I ever would have changed, or decided to take the risk of speaking out. After that, there was no going back. And one thing I was determined to speak – and write about – was this concept of 'the essence of a nobody.' Growing up I was a nobody; I was the very essence of a low-life scumbag. I think you'll have got that from reading this book. The question is, how to stop yourself from being the essence of a nobody. How to rise above all that.

Of course, I did not have a dad or a mother or any adult role model in my life, not before my section commanders in the British Army took on that kind of a role. I did not pick up the life skills I should have done as a child. With the early mental torture, I just took it on the chin as being normal; as if that was what I deserved. That was what everyone told me, and in a searing indictment of the system I did not feel that I could approach anyone for help. I was never allowed to build up a degree of trust with anyone. When I did, it was horrifically abused. I could not confide in anyone about anything at any time – not even to the other kids in the homes, for I did not want to risk getting laughed at or being seen as 'weak'.

When the chief abuser followed me into Civvy Street, I only felt I had finally escaped all that when I joined the Army. But when I lost Charlie, my closest mate in the military, to a senseless accident, I had faced problems again; again, my mental health went into freefall. But I did not breathe a word about it, because I felt it would impact my status in the military. Again, it was the shut up and stay quiet argument – or it'll end badly for you. When I felt I needed to speak to someone most during my military years, my thinking was – *If I come clean about facing mental health challenges, they will bin me.* I would have been out on my ear, and for me the British Army was the only family that I had ever had.

When serving in Northern Ireland with the Royal Hampshires, one of the staff sergeants used to stand in the incident room after any particularly kinetic operation – like when I had got blown up in the pub-bombing incident – and say: 'Anyone have a problem with anything we have just done? If so, you can go see the shrink.' There would be sniggers all around the room. Presented like that, no way was anyone about to raise their hand and say: 'Yeah, actually, I need to go speak to someone.'

During those earliest days in Derry we had a WRVS woman – from the Women's Royal Voluntary Service – put there for our supposed welfare. The NCOs would ask at times – Does anyone want to go see the WRVS? It was always said very sarcastically; tauntingly almost. Almost like – Any of you lot weak pussies, then? You knew at the end of the day how bad it would look, not to mention how badly it would impact your career, if you were the one to break.

I had no family, so I had nobody to turn to or to talk to. When my best mate, Charlie – the closest thing I had ever had to a confidante; to a brother – died in that accident, I went off the rails big time. I started drinking too much; I started fighting all the time;

267

I was trying to mask it with the booze and the punch-ups. Had I felt I could speak about my mental health without getting binned, I would have been able to deal with it. For sure. Eventually, it was that kind of behaviour – untreated; unrecognized; undiagnosed – that led to me having to leave the military.

Admitting to mental health issues was a huge stigma in my mind back then. Even when out of the military, I still believed it would make me unemployable and a no-go on the private military circuit. Before that, the military had instilled the keep-quiet-and-take-all-the-shit attitude, which backed up all that I'd been told in the kids' homes. And always in the back of my mind was the fear that I would never be allowed on SAS selection, if I admitted that I was 'a fucking nutter', which was how we all used to refer to anyone who did 'crack up' back then.

That was the culture at that time. Thank God it's changing.

Since joining the military I have always tried to admit to doing whatever I have done wrong. When I signed up I had it drummed into me – stick your hand up if you've done something wrong; admit it, and you'll be treated fairly. A good example is what happened when I was twenty-two years old, and I went to do the Junior Brecon course, at the Infantry Battle School, in Brecon, Wales.

That first night there was nothing much to do, so several of us on the course hit the town and the beers. We got back to camp late, and realized we'd forgotten the code to the door, to enable us to enter the sleeping quarters. In our inebriated state, it seemed like a good idea to me and my drinking buddy, a guy from the Royal Green Jackets, to kick the door off the hinges so we could get our heads down and get some sleep.

We gathered the next morning, two-three hundred recruits for the course, plus the senior staff officers who were running it. The regimental sergeant major strode in, his face like thunder. 'Sorry to say this, but this course has not started well. Some smart-arse has smashed the doors to the accommodation block off their hinges. So, would the guilty party like to step forward.'

I stood up without really thinking about it. Remember – fess up and it won't go badly for you. I was expecting my drinking 'buddy' to do exactly the same. Not a chance. He sat there immobile, with his arse on his hands. My punishment was to get the door repaired out of my own funds, to pay a fine and to face a verbal dressing down. That was it. Misdemeanour admitted to and promptly forgotten – one of the best things about service with the British military.

That Green Jacket lad thought he'd got away with it. Not a chance. Next time I saw him down town, I walked up to him and without a word of warning or a gesture I head-butted him in the face. He returned to camp with a bloody nose and a couple of black eyes and tried to lodge a complaint. No one was having any of it. They knew he'd kicked the door in, along with me, and that he'd failed to admit to it. They figured he was doubly guilty: 1, for smashing the door in; 2, and, much worse, for letting me take the rap.

Honesty was the best thing – that was what the military drilled into me. But there was the one big exception: the elephant in the room. The unwanted ginger stepchild of service to Queen and Country was mental health. If you weren't of sound mind, it was time to ship out. That was what everyone back in my day felt most and feared most. I like to think it has got a whole lot better. Certainly, the British military needs to be encouraging people to speak out: to open your damn mouth; to not let your mental health overshadow your chances of pursuing your dreams, whatever they may be.

That's what I am endeavouring to do, now. In speaking out as I have, I've received the most uplifting and effusive reactions imaginable. I have received message after message after message from those who say my honestly and frankness – revealing my deepest trauma and my vulnerabilities – has turned their lives around. Let me tell you something – that feels better than any brown envelope stuffed full of cash that anyone could slip into your hand. My background – being a product of the system – makes this all so real. It means I can talk to people from the same kind of place from which I started out. I've been deep down in the mud; I've been there with them on the factory floor.

Which goes back to what I am doing now with my life. If you're a man on his arse bones, who's pulled himself up by his boots straps, you're the one many will relate to. I can genuinely say: 'I've been there; I've felt it – but look how I've turned it around.' I'm fifty-one years old and I'm still not completely out of the woods. I'm still learning. My wife, Wendy, says: 'You're not rich until you're rich in love.' Fine words. All the flash cars and clothes and houses – none of it will make you any better or any happier, not unless you're first sorted inside. Who dares does indeed win – but trust me, it's the battle within that counts most.

As part of winning that battle I've learned not to bear any grudges. I won't bear a grudge against the military for the way they used to approach mental health issues facing those who served, including myself.

In recent weeks, believe it or not someone from a Kingham Hill has actually reached out to me – that's the private school from which 'Council House Kevin' was summarily expelled, for having smashed up the library with the floor buffer. They'd tracked me down on Facebook, and they were after a motivational speaker – who better than the kid who had got thrown out at age fourteen, but who'd gone on to make something remarkable of himself, albeit not without hitting a few speed bumps along the way.

One of my room-mates at Kingham Hill was a guy called Nigel Bartlett. Nigel went on to become a Royal Marine. Of course, I'd been a commando too, and Nigel sure knew who I was today. So when he reached out to me on Facebook, I was more than happy to return the gesture and to offer help. Kingham Hill – like all British schools – had been in lockdown for weeks on end, under the coronavirus restrictions. He wanted me to give a video address in which I could speak about how I'd turned my own lockdown – the life that I'd spent in the kids' homes – into what it is today. I was more than happy to oblige.

I have never sought to bear a grudge. Even with my adoptive father – the man who had smashed my head in as a kid, many, many times – I did not hold a grudge. I went to see him when he was dying in hospital. I could have smashed his head in – payback time. What would have been the point? Instead, I took hold of one of those hands which had seemed so big and gnarled and powerful all those years ago, held it in mine, and told him it was all going to be okay. I did my best to comfort him in his hour of need. I felt better for it. So, I hope, did he. Bearing a grudge – it would only serve to screw me up.

My next big project is going to be to return to Sierra Leone, a country in West Africa where I have spent some considerable time, and which really got under my skin. We'll be making a TV documentary about the British military interventions in Sierra Leone – there have been many, including Operation Palliser, Operation Barras and others, and they've involved a plethora of British military units, including the RAF, the Marines, the Paras, the Royal Irish Regiment and others – and what long-term effects they may or may not have had on that long-suffering country.

The single greatest achievement of the British military in Sierra Leone was to bring to an end the horrific civil war there, which had ravaged the country for over a decade, leaving a nation horribly traumatized. But when we take the cameras in and go back to those key areas in which British troops served, fought, were held hostage and on occasion spilled their blood and lost their lives, I'll want to get right under the story; I'll want to discover: what was it all really for? With the help of the Sierra Leone army (SLA) and some of their veterans, we'll be seeing if, in the aftermath of such military interventions, life has really changed for the better for the locals. In short, we'll be asking – what did British soldiers die for? What were we all fighting for? What was the objective and has it been achieved?

Do the locals even have the basic necessities of life: electricity, clean running water, and access to education? If not why not? Education is key. I know that better than most. I never had any to speak of. I know how that curtailed my prospects and how my life journey has so often involved a struggle to overcome the prejudices of others, because I do not have any fancy letters after my name. Have we brought education to the people of Sierra Leone? Have we fulfilled their burning desire to learn and to better themselves, which would mean that in truth we had really given them back their country? Did we end hostilities there, only to fail to finish the job?

Those are the kind of questions we will be asking. I'll revisit he key military sites, carry out interviews with the key people on the ground, and trust me we'll produce a sizzler of a programme. But that's not enough. I'd love nothing more than to make a real difference – to get some of that development done; to get running water and electric into the villages there; to make a real difference in the lives of some of the poorest people on earth. As we did in Syria, I'll get amongst the people on the ground and tell the in-depth story. This is real hearts-and-minds stuff, and it thrills me.

I'm still fighting the battle within. I guess I always will be. But trust me, in that context who dares to speak out – to break the silence – really does win.